22 YEARS OF HELL

THE ALEXIS PATTERSON STORY

BY
KENYA C.L. CAMPBELL

Feb. 14, 2020

Dear Mr.Campbell,

I am working on a project about your missing daughter, Alexis, and I am writing to ask for your help. First, I want to say how sorry I am about what happened to Alexis. I have been spending a lot of time talking with Ayanna over the past several weeks and I feel I have been learning quite a bit about your daughter. It sounds like she was a wonderful, bright light in both your lives.

The project I am working on is more involved than the typical news stories that have been done over the years. Since 2015, I have been producing a narrative series for the paper and complementary podcast called "Unsolved" that focuses on open cases in Wisconsin. This year, I am planning to focus on Alexis.

To that end, I would appreciate the opportunity to visit you and talk about her and how her disappearance has affected your life in the years since.

My show has been downloaded more than 4 million times by people all over the world. My hope is that by focusing on Alexis' case, we can figure out what really happened to her and bring her home.

I would appreciate the opportunity to come and meet with you. Please let me know if you would be willing to talk with me. You can call me at 414-224-2125, email gina.barton@jrn.com or write to me here:

Gina Barton, Reporter
Milwaukee Journal Sentinel Newsroom 333 W. State St
Milwaukee, WI 53203

I look forward to hearing back from you and hopefully meeting you.

Sincerely,
Kenya Campbell DOC #00251863 Oshkosh Correctional Facility
P.O Box 3310
Oshkosh, WI 54903-3310

March 31,2017

Hello Kenya.

I am John Mercure.
I host the afternoon radio show on WTMJ radio in Milwaukee. We are the #1 afternoon radio news show in Wisconsin.

I am doing a series of reports on the 15th anniversary of the disappearance of your daughter Alexis Patterson. I am sorry that this happened to you and your family.

Your side of the story is important to me. Our listeners would like to hear from you. I don't think you have been given the chance to talk about the disappearance of Alexis. I would like to give you that chance.

Can I please come to the Oshkosh Prison and do an interview with you?
I would like to set up a time with the Warden. Before I can do that, I need to know that you are willing to talk to me.

I will be fair with you.
Can I arrange to come talk to you? Please write me back:
John Mecure WTMJ Radio 720 E Capitol Dr.
Milwaukee,WI 53212

Or call me: 414-967-5227
Thanks John Mecure

So You Can Write Publications, LLC
PO Box 80736
Milwaukee, WI 53208
www.sycwp.com

Publishing date: 9/27/2024
ISBN-13: 979-8-9899762-2-5

Cover design by: www.sycwp.com
Printed in the United States of America

(Note: "The majority of quotations gathered by the author have been frequently in print and/or movie and television, as well as publicly accessible on the Internet; considered public domain. Where possible, the author and publisher have made their best efforts to credit any available sources for them. In the cases where it was uncertain where they first appeared, the information was cited as "unknown" or "anonymous." The information in this book is intended to uplift and inspire all who read it, or who have it read to them. The information quoted was kept as it was found and/or heard by the author, who makes no guarantee that the information one-hundred percent accurate, just that the author intended for it to be beneficial to all who reads it, or has it read to them."

SO YOU CAN WRITE
PUBLICATIONS®

FRUITFUL THOUGHTS

It's been a long time coming and a long time dealing with the day that my soul melted back in May 2002. I've been contemplating on how I would make the number one suspect feel something that would last him for a lifetime. That all ended January 19, 2021 when he was found dead at the age of 52 from a heroin overdose.

I can truly say that I was sad when I heard the news. Not sad that he had died, but sad that he died with the answers that could put me, the Milwaukee Police Department, and the people who loved Alexis in the position to find her. Don't get me wrong because by no way am I a heartless individual, but you have to take into account the circumstances and situations I've been through with dude over the years. They say don't speak ill of the dead so I'll just say that I won't miss him.

His kids got to grow up with their parents, siblings, grandparents, aunties, uncles and cousins. My children and family were deprived of growing up without Alexis, so I hope you understand I feel robbed. I believe in my heart that he was the link to this whole life altering ordeal. Now I'm back to square one. No insight, no direction and no clue.

My thoughts have always been that he knew more than he told, which was the minute I started my own investigation. You know I would love to meet the person who invented the saying "time heals all wounds" because I would tell them how wrong and inconsistent that statement is. Twenty years and counting got me feeling the exact same way as the first day I heard the news Alexis was missing. My life hasn't moved on, I just navigate through it. I can't even say I'm living; I'm just existing to be honest.

A lot of people over the years have asked me if I think Alexis is still alive, and I always do a double take and look at them funny. I tell them that I know she is and to think differently is like giving up hope and that's one thing I can never do. I would have to be shown otherwise to think and I can't even bring myself to say those words. Am I smart? Am I messed up inside, well that question is rhetorical. Am I optimistic that I'll see my daughter again, ABSOLUTELY! Years ago, I was told by a detective that the chances of finding Alexis was slim to none "statistically" speaking he said. Now they say math is a subject that never changes and statistics are based on mathematics, but what do you call beating the odds because that's a part of mathematics also, that's my critical thinking I responded to him. And if that is all I have to go on then I'm good with those odds. I don't care if there's slim to none as long as there's a chance. When it's all over and the smoke clears, I'll be the only one standing continuing the search to find my baby.

Long after the cameras stopped rolling, the interview and the police investigation had halted, it's me, the parent keeping Alexis in the mind and hearts of people, still asking and begging for anybody with information concerning Alexis to come forward. Reporting a crime isn't snitching, it's an honorable thing to do, especially involving an innocent child. Leviticus 5:1 says "anyone refusing to give testimony concerning what he knows about a crime is just as guilty as the person who committed the crime." Please don't be that person, because silence is compliance.

CONTENTS

PROLOGUE

T.G.I.F. is a slogan society uses to welcome the end of the work week and usher in the start of the weekend. Most people see the weekend as a time to relax, take time for a short getaway, or party. I enjoy weekends myself, but Friday, May 3, 2002, I wasn't destined to enjoy the weekend at all. That Friday was the beginning of my world turning upside down. It was the day my daughter Alexis disappeared.

When I was able to talk to a detective on Sunday the 5th, I was flabbergasted after we got the normal formalities out of the way, and he asked me, "Do you sell drugs, and do you owe any outstanding drug debts?" The situation wasn't about me, it was about my precious daughter. So, the question he asked caused me to reveal some innermost secrets about myself. I told him that I did sell drugs and that I did not owe anyone anything! I confided to him that I was purchasing three pounds of (That Killa) marijuana at a time for a little over
$2,000.

I wondered why that was the first question he asked me after our introduction to one another. He never spoke about Alexis running away, or her being abducted by a stranger. He went straight to the drug question, like he knew something I didn't, or that this was the norm for missing black children. He went on to ask me, "when was the last time you saw Alexis?" I told him that it was around the 20th or 21st of February. This book: Twenty-Two Years of Hell recounts my own personal investigation into the disappearance of my daughter.

I hit the streets hard to uncover information concerning Alexis' whereabouts. Engaging major drug dealers and violent murderous gang members, I sought to have my daughter returned to me, despite having to risk my own life to do it. In the first few days after Alexis' disappearance, all I kept hearing was, "The media wants to see you." However, I was in no shape mentally, nor was I in the mood to talk with them. I didn't even speak to Alexis' mother until May 8th, which was several days later. On that day I went over to her house, and when I saw her, I gave her a tight hug. I held her in my arms for a minute, sensing that she was emotionally drained. I kissed her on her forehead and whispered in her ear that she has to be strong because we will find our daughter.

Although I was treated like a suspect during the Milwaukee Police Department's investigation, I went above and beyond when it came to cooperating with them. Truth be told, I never really cared for the police, but I did comply with what they asked of me anyway. My own feelings aside, I wanted to do anything I could to help them find my daughter and bring her home. I was 100% invested in cooperating with them, no questions asked!

My own investigation into Alexis' disappearance has not stopped just because I have not received the answers I have sought from others. I developed my own sources over time, and I have come to one inescapable conclusion. Alexis was a victim of a grown man's actions; the actions of the number one suspect.

As the years passed, and my investigation continued, I received information that I believe to be true and credible from reliable sources. One time a close associate of Alexis' mother confided in me, and you will see why I believed this person. I won't reveal his name, but I will say that he was a god-brother to Alexis' mother. In our conversation he told me that the number one suspect was affiliated with the Murder Mob, a street gang. They are a group of violent, drug sellers, robbers, and murderous individuals that terrorized the streets of Milwaukee. They were also allies with the Ghetto Boys street gang. He entrusted me with the information that one time the Murder Mob had robbed him at gunpoint, and that Alexis' mother used to mess around with the leader. He also said that she and her female cousins and friends used to frequent their house parties.

I remember one time I was shown mug shots of three individuals by a detective. Two of the three I knew of, but the third one I wasn't familiar with. The detective asked me if I had ever seen this third individual before to which I replied that I hadn't. I asked who this guy was, but I was told not to worry about it since I had never seen him before. Sometime later I found out that the guy was actually the leader of the Murder Mob. It so happened that his picture was on the Facebook page of a female acquaintance I used to deal with back in the day. I was looking at pictures of her and her family, which included ol' boy from the mug shot. She posted him as being her baby daddy. I had heard of dude, because his name was ringing in the streets, but I never knew what he looked like. So. I asked her what her kids father's name was. Then when she told me, I made the connection.

I thought back to why the detective had asked me about the dude a few years prior. It seemed to me that it was no coincidence that I was asking about his clique several years later. But what she did wasn't my business, and no big deal.

Still, what intrigued me was the number one suspect's involvement with the Murder Mob. In a particular encounter I had with Alexis' mother, I asked her if the number one suspect was affiliated with the Murder Mob. She said to me with an attitude in her voice, "Why? Who told you that?" I replied, "That's neither here nor there. Was he, or was he not?" She instantly became irate and said, "Naw, he wasn't, but I was!" I thought to myself, why was she so distraught? So, I said, "Look, I'm trying to see what's going on with the ol' boy surrounding our daughter, and what do you mean by you being affiliated with those dudes?!" I already knew that she was, and I was trying to see if she was going to lie to me or not. Make no mistake about it, however, my main inquiry was about the number one suspect.

So, when she made the comment, she did about being affiliated with them, that only validated what her god-brother told me about her and the dudes in question. When she did reply to my aforementioned statement, she went on a rant about what people were saying. What she didn't know was that more than a few of her relatives were confiding in me besides people from the streets. I really wasn't trying to argue with her, but I had to eventually tell her to leave because I was at work at the time.

A high school friend of mine, Dee, had a Cricket Phone store on the corner of 29th and Atkinson. I was employed there as a phone technician, which meant that I activated new customers accounts and processed cell phone bills. I was also a cashier because the store sold food, tobacco products, and some clothing items. The true meaning of a one-stop shop.

I don't know if I was showing too much interest, or becoming too involved in my daughter's disappearance, but I know in my heart that I was doing what I was supposed to be doing as a parent of a missing child. That meant asking all kinds of questions without care or concern about being offended by my inquiries. Also, working with the police department, who had the resources, manpower, and the capability to find Alexis. Then there was my own investigation of course.

I was blindsided by what happened in the days following my conversation with Alexis' mother. I received a message on my Facebook page from her that was appalling to say the least. It was a mystery to me where all this hostility from her had its origin. When I brought to her attention about the number one suspect, she would get combative even though they were no longer married and had separate lives. Yet she was still being very protective of him.

In the message she stated that she didn't want me present at our daughter's vigil, which was coming up in less than a week. She also said that if I did show up, she would have me physically removed. I laughed to myself because she must have forgotten how I warred in the sometimes-wicked streets of Milwaukee.

When I met her, I was being punished for warring in those streets. I had 60 witnesses that saw how I got down and took care of my business. Those witnesses had agreed to testify against me in court if I didn't take a plea. I won't detail the dialogue of our messaging to one another, just know that I was taking a defensive stance to a person that was being offensive.

Everything I had said to Alexis' mother in those messages was true and accurate. However, that being the case, it was apparent that I had struck a nerve. In addition to the message, she sent telling me not to show up at Alexis' vigil, she also went to my Probation Officer and said that I had threatened to beat her up, which was total fabrication! In fact, that accusation she made to my P.O. resulted in a warrant being issued for my arrest. The police came to my residence ready to take me into custody.

Once in jail, my P.O. began her investigation into the allegations Alexis' mother made against me. Fortunately, I did not erase the message Alexis' mother and I exchanged with one another. My P.O. asked me what was going on in the days after those messages were sent when Alexis' mother came in and made her statement to my P.O. I didn't want to tell her about the conversation in the store days prior because that wasn't my P.O.'s business. It was bad enough that the police were in my business for several years already, so I gave her the short version.

I revealed that I had received some disturbing messages from my daughter's mother talking crazy to me and I said some things back, but not one time did I say anything about touching, hitting, or doing any bodily harm to her or anyone else for that matter. Even though she threatened to have me physically removed if I showed up at Alexis' vigil. Then my P.O. asked me for my Facebook account number and password in order to verify my story. I gave them to her without a problem. A few days later I was released and had to report straight to her office. She said that she was sorry for having to inconvenience me, but she had to lock me up when those types of allegations are made because they have to be taken seriously. She also said that she thought Alexis' mother had lied to her about the situation. Then she apologized to me for locking me up based on false allegations causing me to miss the 8th anniversary of Alexis' disappearance. My P.O. did say that she wasn't happy with the content of the messages she read, but she believed that Alexis' mother was a mean person based on what the content of the messages was. So, she said it was in my best interest to sign a no contract order regarding Alexis' mother. I agreed and I signed it. She apologized again for everything that had gone on, gave me my next appointment date, then I left.

I hated that I missed Alexis' vigil, and I hated it even more that her mother lied to my P.O. which put me in a position where I couldn't attend. My problem has never been with her per se, I just always expressed my position, my beliefs, and I stood by them. The problem this time was when she took a defensive stance concerning the number one suspect. I felt that her stance should have been one for Alexis, not him.

I was, still am, a desperate father doing anything I can to assist in bringing my daughter home. I'm not the enemy. I would go to hell and back, against all odds, and the world to oppose anyone who would seek to hinder the return of Alexis. That is what I wanted her mother to understand! In my search for Alexis, people have been beaten up, some have been shot, others have been jailed, and still others have been detained. One person even had a plot to murder the number one suspect over my daughter.

The disappearance of my baby is heart-wrenching, personal, and profound. What follows are the details of my search and investigation into what happened to Alexis.

22 YEARS OF HELL

THE ALEXIS PATTERSON STORY

BY
KENYA C.L. CAMPBELL

INTRODUCTION

My name is Kenya Campbell, and I am the father of Alexis Patterson. To understand and appreciate my daughter's story, I believe that the ones who this book reaches should first get to know something about who I am, and where I come from.

I have never proclaimed to be a saint, nor have I acted like one throughout a large portion of my life. The truth is that to this day, no one from my past has acted like much of a saint either. As children, most of us were defiant to varying degrees. It's all part of growing up, I guess.

Who I am today is not representative of who I was back in my school days, or even beyond. Those times gave my life perspective, and allowed for maturity on my part. I did my best to apply the lessons I learned correctly; along the way I realized how fragile life is. Anything can happen to anyone at any time, so it really hit me over the years how blessed I truly am even to be alive.

Now, I try to live life to the fullest and not take anything for granted. I am also doing my best to be as productive a human being as I can be. Why the change? It is in the midst of my most difficult trial that my life has been transformed. An innocent little seven-year-old girl taught me the value of love and life.

That little girl is my daughter- for which this book is written. She has been missing for years now, but it is in her absence that I have matured the most. It wasn't that way in the beginning of this trial, but it evolved as the years went by. This is the story of my Twenty-Two Years of Hell.

CHAPTER 1

FROM CHILDHOOD TO FATHERHOOD

I grew up in the projects on the northwest side of the city of Milwaukee. This is an environment where single mothers are the norm and they raise their children the best way they can with what they have.

My dad was around sometimes, but it was my mother who made all things happen for the family. She made our house a home. For this reason, I call my mother a single parent. It was her decision to take on the burden of responsibility for our care. She demonstrated what true parental love is.

My mother had me when she was only 14 years old and it wasn't until she was 19 that she married my dad. Then we moved to California and later on we moved to Japan where my brother was born.

What brought us to these places was my father's enlistment in the Marine Corps. I guess having lived in such far-off lands made me a well-traveled child at a young age. However, we would eventually wind up back in Milwaukee after that. Although there were certain elements among my life experiences that I'm not proud of, I didn't view myself as a heartless individual. I'm human, just like anyone else and like anyone else I've made some bad choices that have changed the course of my life in ways I never imagined.

I never thought of myself as being invincible, I just didn't give a damn! Even though I had a good upbringing, I still carried a bad attitude with me for much of my life. I was just one of those kids who had to find out things the hard way, my way.

My mother and I have always been close and for all my life she has done everything in her power to raise my siblings and I the right way. My mother, the one I so dearly love, always had time for me. I can recall when we would go to the movies or have picnics at the lakefront. These and other outings are too numerous to mention here, and added greatly to our family bonding process.

As I got older, I would keep my street business in the streets out of respect for her. I knew it would break her heart if she found out the things I was doing. She had raised me better than the way I was conducting myself; but I felt that I still had to find my own way.

I am truly blessed because a lot of my childhood peers who have gone to prison are still there today. Not to mention the ones who have been murdered or came up missing, never to be heard of again. That could've been me. Things could've been so much worse for me given the fact that I've done everything under the sun you could imagine. However, I was still spared some of the harshest punishments the law and the streets could have inflicted upon me along the way.

At one time I lived by the insane, "Code of the Streets", which had rules such as, "Do or Die", "Eat or Starve", and lastly "Handle Your Business or Somebody Else Will." And as we all know, for the most part not many of us make it out of that kind of life. Some fall short and pass on or the criminal justice system gets a hold of them. Where the sentences they hand out makes them wish they passed on. In prison, I used to refer to such people as "dead men walking", because they would walk all day doing nothing of substance until they died.

As a child, I was exposed to a lot of emotional and physical abuse by my father toward my mother. Since she was thousands of miles from her family when my dad was in the Marines, I guess he thought he could beat her anytime he felt like it. He didn't have to worry about my uncle, who was back in Wisconsin serving time in prison for shooting a man 5 times for just speaking to his girlfriend. My uncle, the man who named me, gave me my first teething ring and who is a 3rd degree black belt, was and still is registered downtown Milwaukee as a lethal weapon with his hands.

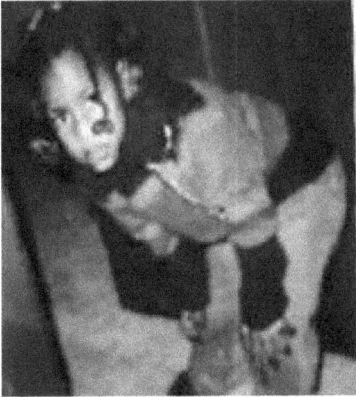

That couldn't help his sisters now that they lived in another state. Yes, I said "sisters", because my mother brought along her baby sister as a babysitter for me and my soon to be baby brother to help her out. My auntie had to be at least 12 or 13 when I was 5 going on 15. I can honestly say that I remember my childhood as if it was yesterday. Hence, I can only imagine what my uncle would have done had he been available to deal with my father.

Back in the 1970's, life was much more laid back and peaceful. 5-year-old children could walk to school without supervision, my friends and I included. In California, I had a white friend and we used to break into other kid's homes when their families weren't home, and steal their toys. These were toys that we had all played with the previous day or earlier in the week, that we had taken a liking to. Now I know you may ask, "how in the world can a pair of 5-year-olds simply break into a house?" Remember when I said that life was laid back and peaceful in the 1970's? Well, it was and people didn't lock their patio doors when they left their homes back then, at least that was true when it came to the parents of the kids I played with. My white buddy and I just pushed the patio door open once we saw a particular family leave their house. We had no fear of getting caught, so when we had taken the toys we wanted, we simply left the same way we came in.

It was funny because we would actually play with the stolen toys with the kids we stole from! And when kids would recognize their toys and say it was his, all I would say is that my mama bought that toy for me and that would be the end of it.

I never saw my mother do anything wrong, or out of the moral context that defined her. So, there I was, a young child left to wonder why it was that my father would cuss her out and be abusive toward her. It must have taken quite a toll on my auntie because she wound up going back to Milwaukee right before we left San Diego for Japan.

Japan was something of another world to me. I had to attend a bilingual school and we lived on the military base. Everything we needed was on the base; stores, restaurants, everything a family needed for living purposes.

I remember my mother getting a job at a cleaning store on the base. She really hit it off with a Latino woman named Theresa; they became real close friends. Theresa had a husband who was also Latino. I don't remember his name, but he looked like Desi Arnaz Jr., the actor and musician who starred opposite his wife Lucille Ball in the classic TV series "I Love Lucy". They were from New York state, and I also remember Theresa watching me a lot during that time. In fact, I used to spend the night at their house more than a few times.

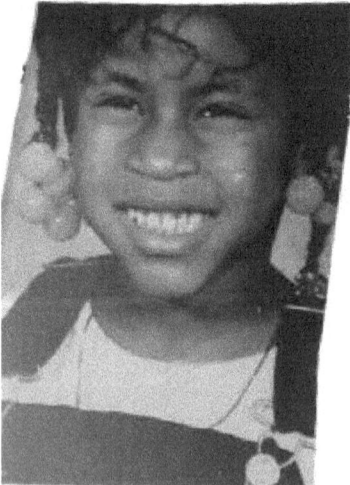

I really didn't like doing that because it was not much different from my own house insofar as the abuse factor is concerned. Theresa and her husband argued in Spanish as a prelude to him beating her up in front of me like I wasn't there. I mean, if I wanted to see a fight like that, all I had to do was stay at home, right? I never understood why my mother sent me over to Theresa's to begin with. Maybe if she knew what was going on over there she wouldn't have. Or maybe she sent me over there to escape all the crap that was going on in our own home, who knows! All I know is that Theresa used to get her butt kicked and being 5 years old, seeing both my mother and Theresa getting their butts kicked by men who claimed to love them can really mess a child's mind up.

I recalled when my brother was born it was the night when I thought my mother was going to die. We were in a military jeep and it was me, my mother, father, and some of his Marine brothers. My mother went into labor and was in pain like I've never seen before. Of course, at my young age I didn't understand the process of labor when it came to having a child so I was just really scared. Anyway, I heard one of the guys say, "Give me a boot string, I have to cut her!" I was in the front seat; my mother and father were in the back and everyone crowded around blocking my view. When dude kept saying, "I got to cut her! I got to cut her!" made me think they were going to kill my mother. As it turned out, my brother had already been born and the guy was talking about cutting the umbilical cord, not killing my mother. But at the age of 5, if you hear anything about someone wanting to cut your mother, you would freak out. I know I did. That was the night of October 7th, 1978.

One night Theresa was watching me and she had a softball game she was playing in that same evening. So, she decided to take me along with her to the game. She bought me a bag of lollipops and told me to sit in this one particular spot so she could keep an eye on me while she was playing. I truly do not know what she was thinking of, buying me what is essentially a bag of sugar and then telling me not to move. That's like taking a kid to Chuck E. Cheese and telling them not to play - ain't gonna happen! Anyway, I was watching the game, but at the same time I was also hopping from bleacher to bleacher. Before I knew it, I was at the very top of the bleachers. Now at this point, I had to be about two stories off the ground, but that didn't stop me from continuing to hop around. That is until my bag of lollipops and I hopped right off the bleachers and landed in the trash can all the way down on the ground. All I remember after that was starting to cry because of the pain and all the people on the ball field running toward me. Then I lost consciousness, and when I awoke, I was in the hospital with my mother and Theresa at my bedside. Fortunately, I only ended up suffering some bruises.

Although I was emotionally abused by the grownups, I was also sexually abused by another child. There was this one black family who lived on the base that were all females; 3 to be exact. A little girl who was my age, her younger sister who was about 1 or 2 years old and her older sister who was around 11 or 12.

When I say there were 3 females in their home, I meant there were 3 siblings in addition to their mother who my mother became friends with. I don't know what it was, something about this older girl that drew her to me, but there was something she found enticing about me. I mean every time we were alone or out of sight from the adults, she would kiss me like I really knew how to kiss, tongue down my throat and all, just like an adult would. I don't know if she found me to be a handsome little boy or what, but she sure didn't mind kissing me all the time. However, when she started touching me on the private part of my body, I was shocked and confused. Not only had nothing like that ever happened to me before, but she was very aggressive with fondling of me - doing it whenever and wherever she wanted.

She manipulated me into keeping quiet about it. It wasn't until now I'm reflecting back on my past for the purposes of this book, that I can speak of it openly. I didn't tell my mother back then because I was ashamed, thinking that somehow, I did something wrong. That's what the older girl did, convinced me that I would be the one who would get into trouble if I told. She would say that it was our little secret. Was she, herself, molested at some point in time and was acting out on what she was exposed to as a young child? I do not know, but it didn't stop until we left Japan and returned to America.

My first real experience with sex with an age-appropriate girl happened in the summer of 1988, when I was living in the Westlawn Housing Project in Milwaukee. I was 14 at the time and I used to lie and say that I had sex before. However, since I really hadn't, I went crazy the first time I ever did it. I mean I was trying to catch up to all the times I said I had sex when I didn't, but I was just fooling myself with all of that. The fact is, some teens start having sex early, some start late, but at the time I didn't know of any who didn't start at all.

Even some of the 'sanctified', that is to say Christian girls from the neighborhood were down with having sex. That was crazy in of itself because their parents were very strict and had them going to church up to 4 times a week. The females that were having sex with guys from the hood seemed to be fascinated by our lifestyles and bored with their own.

The Christian boys even began to do devilish things themselves in an attempt to make an impression on us. It was their way of trying to fit in I suppose. At the same time, they were trying to fit in, they were also trying to hide the things they were doing from their parents who said we were bad influences on them. I ask myself to this day who were the real bad influences on those Christian boys and girls, was it us or the oh so strict parents they had to go home to. I ask this only because as an adult, I look back on those and realize that all the kids who I thought were sanctified, are not practicing those Christian values today. That blew my mind.

Like the old saying goes, you can lead a horse to water, but you can't make him drink. So, like me, those Christian kids had to find their own way.

Also, at 14 years of age I obtained my first firearm- a .22 caliber revolver. My cousin and I stole it from this guy who lived in the projects with us. Actually, the pistol belonged to the guy's mother who was a truck driver and was always on the road. That was the first time I had seen a lady drive an 18-wheel tractor-trailer rig.

We stole the gun from this guy after he showed it to us while it was on his hip. My cousin said to me, "Let's take the dude's gun from him." I said, "How? We gonna jump him or something?" My cousin replied, "Naw, watch this." Then he turned around and said to the guy with the gun, "Hey, I bet you can't beat me wrestling." My cousin then grabs the guy and starts wrestling with him. As they wrestled, my cousin reached under the guy's shirt and grabbed the pistol off his hip and tossed it into the bushes nearby. The guy says, "Wait, the gun fell off of my hip." Then my cousin puts the guy in a headlock and turns him away from where the bushes are. Then he asked me to retrieve the gun from the bushes and I complied. My cousin then releases the guy from the headlock and tells him that we will help him look for the gun. Of course, we don't find it and the guy tells us that his mother is going to beat his butt when she returns home. Then the guy left to go home.

My cousin said to me, "You keep it, it's yours." That same pistol that we stole almost killed me weeks later. My brother Jay, who was nine at the time, had woken up before me one morning prior to he and I departing for school. Jay had evidently reached under my mattress and taken the gun and I was awakened to the sound of a pop. When I jumped up, I saw the gunpowder in the air and Jay lying face down in the bed with the gun in his hand. I was in a panic and scared to death. I thought my little brother had shot himself in the head and was dead.

The only thing I could think of doing at that moment was to holler his name. When I did, he turned his head in my direction with a frightened look on his face. I immediately snatched the gun away from him and hid it in my dresser drawer. Then, after taking care of my personal hygiene and getting dressed for school, I started to make my bed, I happened to notice a bullet hole right by my pillow and I thought, "Damn, here I thought my little brother killed himself, but in actuality, he thought that he killed me." For some reason, our mother didn't hear the gun go off that morning, but she found it later after I went to school.

My mother was putting clean clothes in my dresser when she discovered it. Needless to say, she and my dad made me get rid of it. They took me to see someone my father knew and we sold it to him.

High School was a coming-of-age time for me. It was certainly a dramatic change from both elementary and middle school. While still in elementary school I began rapping. That was in 6th grade and continued into middle school where I had the opportunity to perform in the school talent show. By the 9th grade I was already known as a rapper. I went by the name K-Rock and myself and a friend of mine teamed up to form our own group. We would battle other rappers quite often and never lose; we were that cold. We also performed in our high school talent show our freshman year. Our group garnered a lot of respect for our achievements as underclassmen. Ordinarily, freshman students didn't get any respect of any kind in any high school, no matter what they accomplished.

This was a big deal for us to be able to go to a school with 2,500 kids and not only to know the ones we attended middle school with or other neighborhood kids, but to have all 2,500 kids know who we were was huge. It did not matter whether it was at lunch, in the hallway, at a basketball or football game, we were recognizable. It was all a very overwhelming experience that defies description. But it felt great and it was adding to the arrogance that was coming about in me.

31

10th grade was another year in which I learned something new away from the classroom. Another guy that was in my class, who later had a baby with one of my cousins, taught me how to steal cars of all things. I did start working at McDonald's in the middle of my 10th grade year. However, it wasn't long before my newfound interest in stealing cars and my job crossed paths.

Once a year we had to take a series of final exams at school. For a whole week the exams were given and during that week we had school for half-days only. On one of those days, myself and some other guys went to the McDonald's I worked at for something to eat. There were about 8 or 9 of us. After we ate, we decided to steal a car that was parked out in the lot. Mind you, I had to be back to work in 2 hours since I only had a half-day of school. Nevertheless, we stole the car and drove around until it was time for me to begin my shift at work. I was even dropped off for work in that car. A pretty bold move on our part. One of my coworkers told me that someone just had their car stolen 2 hours before. It was ironic that this would be the first thing I heard when I walked in the door at work. I said that was messed up and then continued to work. I thought to myself, "Y'all some stupid (we'll say 'people' for book purposes). How can a whole restaurant filled with customers and employees not see anything happen?" But it did and that was that.

Not only did I peel cars up, but my cousin, some friends from the neighborhood and myself used to take people's cars that they would leave running in the winter to warm up. In fact, we would walk for hours looking for cars for months at a time and ride them until they broke down on us or the police found them.

My bold and illegal behavior didn't end there. I also went to jail in the 10th grade on 2 counts of strong-armed robbery. It was the first time I had ever been in jail. This was all part of a clique I started called D.G.F., which stood for Don't Give a Fuck. It had about 20 or so members that comprised its total complement.

One day we left school early and went up to another high school, which we often did. When we went to those other schools, we did so to see what kind of girls went there or what kind of trouble we could start. The school we went to on this particular day was on the east side of town. We did what we would normally do, but as we were leaving, we saw these 2 white boys wearing team jackets.

Before I knew it, all the D.G.F. members that were with us rushed the 2 boys and attacked them. They beat them bloody and took their team jackets.

The following week, the police came to our school picking up people every day for a whole week. I was one of the last to get picked up that week. The police picked me up on Friday and on the way downtown, we stopped at a Cousins Submarine Sandwich Shop on Wells St. They left me handcuffed in the back of the squad car as they proceeded to get something to eat. When we got to the police station, they put me in a cold room for hours. When they finally returned, they talked to me about the attack a week prior. After they talked to me, I was taken to another room where I saw one of my homies. We were chained together and transferred to the Detention Center for Youth. I went to court the next morning and was released into the custody of my mother. That was February 14, 1990. I later took a plea for receiving stolen property and was given 2 years probation.

How we got caught was one of our clique members dropped his lunch tickets at the scene of the attack. Lunch tickets had our names and the name of the school we went to on them. People from our school were getting picked up every day because someone else would give a different name to the police about who was involved in the attack.

In the summer of 1991, I had just finished 11th grade and I was still dealing with the mother of my first child who I met the summer before. A friend of mine introduced us; he and I were working at Mcdonald's at the time. He was dating her God-sister when we met.

However, this pales in comparison to the other events of that summer. For instance, my mother was working for the University of Wisconsin in Madison that summer and only came home on the weekends. My grandma kept my siblings during the week for my mother, so a cousin of mine and I had a house to ourselves that whole summer, except the weekends. You can only imagine the kind of wild things that went on in that house during that summer. Not only did I really get into girls, but I got back into pistols as well. Pistols and a hot-head don't mix. So, as you may have already guessed, my first baby's mother wasn't the only girl I was into that summer.

Then there was what transpired between my mother and father that summer. They must have had a misunderstanding of some sort during that time. I mean, it must have been something even more serious than that because my father actually brought another woman to our home one night to fight my mother.

I was in my room talking on the phone when I heard the doorbell ring. About 5 minutes later I heard the door slam real hard. So, I jumped up and ran downstairs to find my mother breathing hard with a busted lip. Angered and shocked, I asked what happened. She told me that my father had brought his bitch over to the house to fight her. My mother said, "I was whipping her butt until your father stepped in and held me down for this woman to gain the upper hand." I then asked if she knew where this woman lived and my mother said she did. She told me the woman lived upstairs at the corner house on 49th and Capitol Dr. With that in mind, I called one of my homies that had a car for a ride. I told him the deal and within 10 minutes he was at my house with his gun.

I had to have access to my homie's gun because I had previously lent mine to a friend for a situation he had to deal with.

We went to the house my mother indicated but I didn't see my father's car right away. So, we went into an alley around the back of the house and there was my father's car next to the garage, out of sight from the street. I told my homie to drive down the street a couple of blocks and wait for me while I handled my business. I got out of the car and walked to the front of the house, which was on a pretty busy street mind you and fired repeatedly into the house until the clip was empty. I took off running back to where my guy parked his car but he wasn't there. So, I ran a couple of more blocks, trying to get out of the area fast.

Suddenly, my homie pulls up in his car to a screeching halt. I jumped in and asked him where he had gone. He told me that when I began shooting, he heard the shots but evidently so did some police who passed by him at the same time. They raced toward the direction of the shots and that's when he took off. At this point I told him to go to my auntie's house, which was a few blocks away in the projects known as Parklawn.

We pulled up to my auntie's house and jumped out of the car. The police were coming up fast down the street with their lights off. I quickly threw the gun in the bushes and then rang my auntie's doorbell like a mad man. By this time, the police had stopped and were shining their spotlight on us. I thought we were caught but after a few seconds they rode off. My auntie opened the door and we went inside. I told her what had happened with my mother and what I had just done. We chilled for a while, then I went outside and retrieved the gun from the bushes. I gave my auntie the gun and told her I would be back later to get it.

From my auntie's house I went to my homie's place and then I finally walked home. Once there, I took a shower to try and get all the gunpowder residue off of my hands and body. I even threw the clothes I had been wearing that night away. Then I went to my room and got back on the phone as if nothing had happened.

My mother did get some payback of her own a couple of weeks later when she spotted my father's car a few blocks away from that woman's house. She set his car on fire, destroying it completely. However, my father's mother bought him another car shortly after that.

The wild events of 1991 didn't stop there unfortunately. I got shot 2 different times that year. Once in August and again in December. In August I was at this one girl's place and she told me that she was pregnant. I knew she was lying and as it turned out later on, the baby was proven not to be mine. But when I got to her place, there was another guy there already. He left after I arrived, so she and I were talking for a little while. Then my mother began to page me repeatedly. I called home and she said that some Latino man kept coming around the house looking for my little brother. He was 12 at the time.

This Latino man was telling my mother what he was going to do to my brother because he had apparently stolen something off his porch. I assured my mother I was on my way home and I bolted out of that girl's place as fast as I could. When I made it home, I chilled and waited to see if the man would return at some point. He actually did come back, only this time I answered the door.

Instead of letting him into the house, I stepped outside and closed the door behind me. There I was ready to shoot this man to protect my brother. I was standing on one side of the porch and he was on the other. An argument ensued between us and he asked me what I wanted to do. Right then I hit him in the mouth and he stepped back and pulled out a 12-inch butcher knife that looked like a smaller version of a machete. As I reached for my pistol in my waistband, I fell back into the bushes behind me and the pistol landed in the grass. I rolled out of the bushes and reached for my pistol. Then I looked over my shoulder and saw the Latino dude over me with the knife, attempting to stab me. Suddenly out of nowhere, I was pulled about 20 feet from the grass into the street by my cousin who appeared out of the blue. He helped me to my feet and lifted my shirt up to see if I was stabbed. I wasn't stabbed but the guy came at me again with the knife. As he swung the knife wildly, I ran in circles trying to avoid the blade. A friend of mine who witnessed the whole thing came into the picture and asked me where my pistol was. Still dodging the swings of the knife, I said it was up by the bushes and to hurry up and get it.

Then I started to run down the street. Behind me the Latino guy was chasing me with my homie and my cousin chasing him. All of a sudden, I heard shots ring out. Pop! Pop! Pop! Pop! I felt a pinch in the back of my neck that began to burn really bad. Damn, my homie got the guy off of me but he shot me in the process! I walked back toward my homie and my cousin and they ran up to me. I said to my homie, "Folks, you shot me!" He must have been in shock, hoping he did not shoot me but he really wasn't sure. He said "A shell hit you, a shell hit you!" Then when I reached back and put my hand on the back of my neck, I showed him my hand covered in blood. He began to sob dramatically. I told him not to trip about it, as they walked me the 50 feet or so to my house.

My mother came out, saw me and then started to scream loudly as she held me in her arms. I saw my little brother running up the street, then I passed out in my mother's arms. When I woke up, I was in the hospital.

My cousin had to run home to get his pistol to go hunt down the Latina dude to shoot him. He wound up going to jail that night for disorderly conduct because he was so hysterical over the fact that I got shot. Ironically, my homie who shot me also went to jail that night.

In the jail downtown, my cousin saw one of our neighborhood friends who had just shot 2 men, killing one, down at the lakefront. One of the men he shot had shot at him previously when he had his baby son with him. That served as the motive for the shootings. It's also why the lakefront closes earlier now than it used to. I met up with him myself when I went to prison later on. He was hard on me because he loved me and wanted me to go back into the world a better man with my priorities straight. His concern was not only for me but for my son as well. By me becoming a better man that would allow me to pass on those life lessons to my son. Thus, this would break the cycle of criminal behavior that prevailed in my life to that point.

Now back to what happened in August 1991. I was treated and released from the hospital after regaining consciousness. The district attorney called me the following day, asking if I wanted to press charges. I said no and my homie got released later that day. After his release, he came straight over to see me and apologized for shooting me. I told him not to trip about it but next time watch where the hell you're aiming at and we both laughed. Well, I at least tried to laugh but if I moved my neck too much it hurt. In December, 4 months after I was shot the first time, I was shot again. It was in front of my house and it all began when my neighbor wanted to see a new pistol that I had. My neighbor was with another guy who also wanted to see the pistol. I let my homeboy see it but told him not to put a bullet in the chamber.

However, he did so anyway. So, I made a comment calling him a hard-headed mother or something of that nature. A continuation of the word 'mother' comes to mind. Then I told him to give the pistol back to me. As I reached for the gun from directly in front of him, I heard a shot being fired followed by the ominous sight of feathers flying out of my team jacket. My stomach started to burn and I realized where I got hit. I could not even walk. Another one of my homeboys, James Earl, pulled up and saw me bleeding. He snapped and was about to shoot the guy who shot me but the police were some 50 feet or so away and approaching fast. So, he took my pistol, jumped in his car and left. My mother was told and once again she came out of the house crying, saying, "Oh my baby! Oh, my baby! What happened? Who did this?"

But the guy that shot me took off before I could point him out to my mother.

When I got to the hospital, the police came to my room to talk to me after the doctors fixed me up. They wanted to know who shot me. I told him I didn't know who did it. Obviously, I did know but I wanted to handle this cat if my guys didn't get him first. The police said they thought I was lying. They said they found bullet casings in front of my house but since only one shot was fired in this incident, then the other casings were from another time. However, the police persisted with this line of questioning, saying that I had a shoot-out with this guy who shot me. We argued about the point for about 15 minutes before they left my room. As they were leaving, one of them said that they were going to get a kit in order to test my hands for gunpowder residue. I told them to do what they needed to do - then they left and never returned.

I was released from the hospital and the next day the chump who shot me got my number from my neighbor and tried to apologize for shooting me. I attempted to let him know that everything was okay and to come over to see me. He said he would but he had moved out of town a few days after he shot me. My guys had put the screws to him and scared him out of town before I got well. Now I was mad for 2 reasons: 1. I got shot and I wouldn't get any payback for it, and 2. My Chicago White Sox team jacket was all messed up now because of the bullet that tore a hole in it and my blood that stained it.

Every person has their share of good and bad times and some of those bad times are tragic. The events of my life I've shared here are mostly of the tragic variety. That was by design because it is in those moments where I have learned my greatest lessons. Now begins the part of the story where I transition from Childhood to Fatherhood. Specifically, becoming a father to my precious daughter Alexis.

CHAPTER 2

INNOCENT

It was the winter of 1993, between the months of February and March. I was 19 years old working at a Cousins Submarine Sandwich Shop at 42nd and Villard Ave in Milwaukee.

One night I was working and I noticed a light-skinned female enter the shop to order some food. I thought she was very attractive as I watched her joke around with one of my coworkers. After she left, I asked my coworker if he knew her personally and he told me he did. With my curiosity piqued, I asked him the next time he spoke to her to ask her if I could have her phone number. He did something even better than that; about 15 minutes later he called her and explained to her who I was and that I would like her phone number. She told him to give me her number and that is what he did.

A year and a half later she became the mother of my precious daughter, Alexis Sheree Patterson.

In January 1995, I had a mishap that resulted in being sent to jail for driving after revocation. I had picked up Alexis' mother from a doctor's appointment at St. Joseph Hospital. At the time she was still pregnant with Alexis.

As I made my way through traffic, a car ran a stop sign and hit us, sending my car onto the sidewalk where it came to rest on a fire hydrant. Alexis' mother and I were taken to the same hospital we had just left, with minor injuries. But thank the Lord, Alexis' mother was fine. After I was treated, I was transported to jail. Ironically, I was also in jail with Huber privileges when I first met Alexis' mother a year and a half earlier for shooting at some guys off a Milwaukee County City Bus, even though we only talked briefly when we first met, our rapport with one another intensified in the late spring of 1994 between May and June.

Now I was back in jail because of the accident and I didn't get out until April 5th, 1995, one day after Alexis was born into this unpredictable and sometimes cruel world.

After her birth, I asked plenty of questions as one would when it comes to having a newborn, for instance, what's her weight? Length? Her color? Since I am brown-skinned and her mother is light-skinned. How much pain did she have? Who was in the delivery room? Etc.., etc. During our conversation it seemed that Alexis' mother was getting tired so I told her to get some rest and call me again when she felt better.

At this time, I was confined to my home under house arrest, so I wasn't permitted to go anywhere. I didn't get a chance to see Alexis for the first time until a few weeks later on Mother's Day. Alexis' great grandma, Ms. Betty, brought Alexis, her mother, and a couple more relatives over to see me that day. Ms. Betty was a very sweet lady. I see where Alexis got that trait from.

When I saw Alexis for the first time that day, I saw a reflection of myself in her face and I felt so proud. Both for her mother and for myself. She was so tiny with hardly any hair, but she sure had a beautiful smile. When I held her in my arms that first time, I felt an immediate bond with her, just as I did with all my other children.

When she was born, Alexis was the smallest of all my children born before her. So, I wanted to make sure that her health was good. As I looked into those itty-bitty eyes, I wondered what her life would be like, but I had a strong feeling that one day she was going to make a tremendous impact on the world. Those were just a couple of thoughts that I pondered as I held her tiny frame in my arms as I gently gave her precious kisses upon her forehead and her little lips.

The first time I changed Alexis' diaper was on Mother's Day also. And it was a stinker!!! It's funny now as I look back and remember the little grunt sounds, she was making, as well as the facial expressions. As I was changing her diaper, she probably wondered why I was making that screwed up face as I cleaned her up. Nevertheless, I was so full of pride and joy that she was there and so very thankful that Ms. Betty had taken the time to bring Alexis over to allow me to bond with her. It was a profound couple of hours that I had to spend time with her that day.

For Alexis' first birthday I bought her several pink outfits and gave her mother some money for her as well. Actually, I gave the money to one of Alexis' mother's relatives to give to her because I didn't see her before I left the party.

There is a special bond that exists between fathers and daughters. There is nothing like it. The time with Alexis at the party proved that. There were kids and grown-ups, but mainly a lot of women in Alexis' mother's family. Alexis received a number of gifts that day and all were well-deserved. I sensed that she was enjoying the fact that she was the center of attention. Seeing all her cousins and the adults cater to my precious gem only validated my initial feelings from a year earlier, that she was going to make quite an impression on the world at some point.

I had never been to a party where the birthday child was held and then passed to everyone who attended. It was special and intriguing all at the same time. Alexis was royalty to them! I was blown away and oh, so proud at that moment. Before I left that day, I told Alexis what a sweet and special baby she was and that I loved her dearly.

I was so blessed to have Alexis in my life for the 7 years God allowed us to have. Even though we had awesome and loving times together, I have to admit that there were two situations I wished she hadn't witnessed.

I'll recall one now and elaborate on the other later on because Alexis was a few years older by then. One hot summer day in 1997, when Alexis was 2 years old. Alexis and her sister Special, who was also 2 years old, only a couple of months younger than Alexis. Irene, my pit bull terrier and myself were over at my mother's home at 5th and Vienna St. This was a warm and summer day and to cool off we stayed in the house watching the Cartoon Network under the fans in my mother's room. I don't know why my mother had a cable in her room and not in the living room, which had a big TV but that's how she had it. I once asked her about that and she simply said, "I don't be in the living room." If you ask me, I think it was my mother's way of maintaining a bond and interacting with her children and grandchildren. If we wanted to watch something of interest that regular TV wasn't showing, like a movie, we had to go to my mother's room. The TV in the living room had a VCR I might add.

So, as we watched cartoons, Irene came and jumped up onto my mother's queen-sized bed with us. I noticed that she smelled a little foul, so I told her to lay on the floor with the intent of washing her up when the cartoon we were watching was over. When the cartoon ended, I took Irene into the bathroom, placed her in the tub, ran some lukewarm water, lathered her up and began to scrub away. After rinsing Irene and drying her off, I took her outside and chained her up in the backyard.

I then went back inside the house and got a towel from the linen closet, then a neckbone off the stove where my mother had been cooking a pot of neckbones and potatoes earlier. I tied the neck bone inside the towel, then I went back outside to train Irene in attack tactics, which I did quite often.

This was the process by which I let Irene smell the neck bone inside the towel, then unchained her and held the towel in the air for her to jump up and lock down on the towel, trying to get the neck bones out of the towel on my command. Much like a game of tug-of-war. If she was successful, she would then be rewarded with the neck bone. However, if she couldn't tear the towel open and retrieve the neck bone, then there was no reward.

As I trained Irene, Alexis appeared at the back door and was banging on the screen like she wanted to come outside with me. So, I pulled Irene over with me to the door because we were still engaged in our tug-of-war ordeal. Then I opened the door for Alexis to come out.

While she was outside with me, Alexis made an attempt to try and touch Irene as I was tugging and Irene was pulling but I quickly stopped her in her tracks. I didn't want to have to kill my dog for biting my daughter. So, I told Alexis to stand back and I put Irene back on her chain in the yard. Irene never bit me or anyone else in my family for the time that I had her but I just wasn't taking any chances. As much as I loved my dog, I would've shot her dead if she bit me or any of my children. I picked Alexis up and took her back into the house with me.

I asked Alexis if she wanted to go to the store with me and she nodded yes. I said okay and told her to let me go so I could give Irene a bowl of water before we left. I took care of Irene, then got Alexis and Special and went out the back door to the store.

We walked over by the fence and I unchained Irene so she could go with us. There were 3 stores in the vicinity of my mother's house. One was on the corner of 3rd and Keefe St. Another was on the corner of 4th and Vienna Ave. and the last store was on Port Washington Road between Melvina and Abert. I decided to take them to the store on Port Washington Road. When we arrived at the store, I tied Irene up to a pole. In actuality, I wrapped her chain up and made a knot. Once inside the store, I bought Alexis and Special some candy. Slow poke suckers for Alexis and chips for Special which they both loved anytime, all the time. In addition, I bought both of them 25 cent juices.

When we came out of the store, I heard my name being called by a guy I'll refer to as Wood. Wood was a pretty cool and quiet dude from the neighborhood. Years later I learned that his sister used to date an associate of a man I'll call the number one suspect. He was Alexis' mother's husband at the time. More on why I address him as the number one suspect later on.

Wood's sister was seen being thrown out of a van when it came to an abrupt stop. Then the van took off down the street. Once Wood's sister got to her feet and collected her thoughts after being introduced to the street pavement, she proceeded to walk up the block. People who saw this horrific scene asked her if she was alright and if she needed help. I'm sure she was afraid or maybe even embarrassed but she declined help and continued walking.

Then the van pulled back around the block and stopped beside her. She spoke with the occupant for several seconds before getting back in the van, never to be heard from again. It was ironic to me that this woman would come up missing at the hands of a guy who was a friend of the last person to be seen with Alexis when she came up missing; A.K.A. the number one suspect.

I untied Irene and the four of us walked toward an apartment I used to live in that was two houses and an apartment building from the store we had been at. We talked about a situation, about something he wanted to purchase from me and I told Wood that I would be back in 20 minutes. I didn't have the construction job I once had in Germantown but I'm surviving in the streets. Before we left, I decided to carry Alexis and Special because I had something to prepare. I had Alexis in my right arm and Special in my left arm, with Alexis holding the chain for Irene.

As we were leaving the apartment building, the owner, who was my ex-landlord, came out. He told me he wanted to talk with me for a second.

I stopped to talk with him and he began talking about some damages to the carpet in the unit I used to rent from him. I told him that I'll be back to talk with him about it as soon as I drop my daughters and my dog off at home. In all honesty, that was my intention but I guess that wasn't what he wanted to hear because he punched me in my face while Alexis and Special were in my arms. I was totally mortified! I backed up so I could put them down and in the process of doing that, Wood, who saw what happened, hit my ex-landlord one time and backed off of him as he fell. My ex-landlord tried to get up but it was too late. By that time, I had already put Alexis and Special down and I was furious. I shouted, "Wrong answer mutha fucka!" Then I hit him and knocked him on his butt. After that I put my hands on him and punched until I couldn't punch anymore. My hands were numb with pain and when that happened, I began kicking and stomping him. Even Irene joined in and bit him.

In all the chaos, I just happened to look up and saw Alexis and Special crying. I left Irene with my ex-landlord and went over to them. That's when this female from the hood, I'll call her Red, came over and said, "Ken, I got your babies. You go get your dog."

Alexis and Special had to be terrified after what they had just witnessed. The way they were crying made me angrier, so when I got Irene off the landlord, I punched him a few more times as he lay motionless on the ground. He was still alive because I could see his chest moving up and down.

As I walked over to Red and my daughters, I was beginning to drag my right leg because I was feeling pain in my right foot. Red was holding Alexis and Special in her arms and the chain for Irene but she still managed to escort me to my mother's house. As we left the area, someone yelled, "What happened to ole boy?" Red, who was an imposing figure in all the right places, retorted, "Don't worry about it! It's a G-D business!"

The five of us made it to my mother's house and went inside. I told her what happened and then took my shoe off to show her my foot. When my mother saw that my foot was twice its normal size, she immediately got up to take me to the hospital. I thanked Red for all she did during the incident with my former landlord and I told her to call me in a few hours. I intended to look out for her when I returned from the hospital like she did for me.

My sister Nicole, who was 15 years old at the time, watched Alexis and Special for me while our mother took me to the hospital. There they took X-rays of my foot which showed no broken bones, but I did suffer a bone bruise. I was on crutches for 6 weeks. Although the swelling went down after two weeks my foot was sore the whole time I was on crutches.

I later learned that my ex-landlord had spent a few days in the hospital himself. I had beat him to the point that he didn't even recall what he had done. However, after the incident, I wondered what effect the whole thing would have on Alexis and Special. Alexis had never seen me hostile or upset at any human being before this. She only knew me as being a loving father to her. Now to see me in a fit of rage made me think years later that when I had seen her crying that day, that she must have been scared and confused about the situation and how I reacted to it. True enough, I could have walked away after my ex-landlord hit me but I was young and not as mature as I am today. At the time I was thinking to myself that this guy must be crazy to do what he had just done to me. He hit me in my face, with my daughters in my arms. He showed no regard for their safety or well-being. What if his punch had been more forceful and knocked me out?

What if he had missed me and struck one of them? All he could think of was himself and trying to embarrass me in front of all who were watching. Those were my immediate thoughts and I reacted on impulse. After I put Alexis and special down, all I could think about doing is setting this guy straight. I'm not proud that Alexis was exposed to that confrontation and I wish I would have handled it differently but unfortunately it happened the way it did and I can't change that. Since that time, I have forgiven my former landlord.

I love all my children with all my heart. They all have their own distinctive personalities but I show no favoritism between them. I deal with them as individuals. Alexis was always a sweet child and got along well with her siblings.

At present I have 11 children in all but at the time of Alexis disappearance, I had 8 children, 4 residing in a different household. However, I always made it my business to get them all together on weekends so we could bond as a family.

We would go to the park and the store: I cooked for them, we watched movies together and I ordered out for food when I didn't feel like cooking. Alexis especially liked pizza. I would say something like, "Alright y'all, what do y'all want to eat?" And Alexis would be the first one to shout out, "Pizza! Ooh, pizza daddy, pizza!" She would crack me up with the face she made when she said it.

I can't forget all the wrestling matches we used to have either. To make things somewhat even, I would get down on my knees but they were like an army of little soldiers on D-Day. Every time I threw one of them on the couch or flopped one of them down on the bed, another courageous little one would replace their fallen comrade. However, to my surprise, Alexis figured out her own strategy in subsequent contests. While I was busy handling 2 or 3 of her siblings, she would jump on my back and cover my eyes with her hands. Then came all those tiny punches from all directions. This was one of many memorable times we had as a loving family.

Alexis was such a wonderful child. She never gave me a hard time or attitude when she was told to do anything. She wasn't the type of child that needed discipline and she never fought with her siblings. Whenever Alexis came over, I was always fascinated by how seriously she took her role as a big sister to her baby brother K.J. She would pick him up and place him on her little hip and then carry him around the house. It was moments like that I have always treasured in my heart.

When Alexis was 5 years old, I was residing on 9th street between Center St. and Clark St. I was still rapping and doing shows. On the weekends, when Alexis and her siblings would come over, they would stay up late because I never told them to go to bed. They used to watch scary movies but there was one particular video they loved to watch that wasn't a scary movie at all. I would see them watching it on different occasions week after week. It was a video of my childhood friends and I in the studio recording raps. I don't know why Alexis and her siblings liked it so much but every time they would come over to my house they would watch it before sunrise the next day. Actually, they watched it more than I did.

I honestly felt that Alexis loved to come over to the house on a regular basis and looked forward to it because she always had playmates and of course her daddy was super cool. We always had a good time laughing, playing, bonding and just loving each other.

In August of 2000, my niece was turning a year old and to celebrate there was a birthday party planned for her downtown at a children's play-place. The play-place was located in a high-rise building. It was sort of like Chuck E. Cheese, but we did not have to pay to play the games, like we have if we were at an actual Chuck E. Cheese. As usual I gathered all of my kids for the festivities.

When Alexis was brought over, she had a cast on her left arm. I asked her mother about it and she told me that Alexis fell off a porch or through the porch banister something to that effect. Whatever it was, all I could focus on was that my baby's wrist was broken. I didn't believe the story her mother told me because she wasn't sure of her facts.

When I was alone with Alexis, I asked her what happened to her wrist. Alexis told me that she fell through the porch, not off the porch and no mention of a banister. But when she told me this, she had her head down, not looking me in the eye like she always did when she spoke to me. So, I gently told her that she could tell me anything and didn't have to be afraid, as I held her cast and kissed her fingers. Again, Alexis repeated to me that she fell but I suspected that she had been coached to tell me or anyone else who asked about her injury, that Alexis' mother wasn't present when Alexis had her accident and I believe that she was told what had happened from the person incharged with her care at the time. However, in the grand scheme of things, the whole situation didn't sound right to me. Several years after Alexis' disappearance, I was told by a relative of her mother that the one I have referred to as the number one suspect was responsible for her broken wrist. But by that time, I had lost track of him. He was not living on 49th and Garfield Ave or 44th and Vliet St. or 42nd and Bonnie St.

Although Alexis spent a lot of time with her siblings and extended family members, the 2 of us had our time alone together. One time Alexis was in K-5, her mother called me and asked if I could pick Alexis up from school. The school was part of a church on the corner of Sherman Blvd. and

North Ave. When I arrived to pick her up, she was in class participating, which made me proud. I knew she was smart but seeing her in class and interacting with her teacher made it all the more real to me.

One of her teachers told Alexis that it was time for her to go. Then she looked up and saw me and she instantly smiled. She said, "Hi daddy" and I said, "Hi baby." Then she got up, grabbed my hand and we walked over to the location where the students placed their book bags. Alexis then showed me her work that she had completed that day, a drawing of the sun, clouds, a house with grass and people smiling. I told her I loved it.

In the summer of 2001, Alexis was 6 years old when me, my son Kierre, who was a few months older than Alexis, Special and Alexis herself were visiting my mother on 5th St. My two youngest sisters, Angela and Alisha, who were 12 and 11 at the time, took them to the store on 4th and Vi- enna after I had given them all some money. When they returned from the store, Kierre had blood on his hand and all over his t-shirt. Upon seeing the blood, I panicked. Frantically, I asked what happened to him. They all told me that this little boy had bumped Alexis while skipping ahead of her in line at the store, causing her to drop the snacks she had in her arms on the floor. As Alexis bent down to retrieve her items, the boy kicked some of them. Kierre then punched the boy in the face, busting his nose and then put him in a headlock. That's how the blood got on his t-shirt. I asked Kierre why he did that and his response was, "Don't anybody mess with my sister!"

If Alexis could foster a protective instinct in her brother at such a young age, imagine what she was going to do as an adult. Alexis wasn't a problem child nor did I ever have to physically discipline her. I've always been laid back with my children. I did what was necessary to bring them up right but that didn't mean I needed to be heavy-handed about it. When it came to parenting Alexis, her mother wasn't as lax as I was. If I had to find one word to describe her parenting style, I would say strict or concrete.

So, I didn't believe the story that Alexis had a temper tantrum the morning of her disappearance. It was told to me that she had a temper tantrum because she couldn't bring treats to school for her classmates. The way I looked at it, if I was laid back with her and I had no problems with her, how could her mother - a no-nonsense parent - have such a problem with her over some treats? Alexis knew what her mother expected of her and how her mother chose to parent her. I firmly believe that the whole story about Alexis having a temper tantrum and running away because she couldn't take cupcakes to school as a treat for her class was made up. Just as the story about how Alexis broke her wrist was so fabricated.

The number one suspect stated that he hoped she ran away because she got punished that morning for not doing her homework the night before. Now there is not only a claim that Alexis had a temper tantrum and ran away, but she also didn't do her homework either.

This is a child who the teacher said was a pleasure to have in class and was so sweet, yet the number one suspect states that she didn't do her homework. A sweet little girl that now is said to have a temper tantrum the morning she disappeared. Then there might be the most telling clue of them all to Alexis' disappearance - the number one suspect stating that he hoped Alexis ran away - a clear indication that he didn't want her around. And for a child that was supposedly punished for not doing her homework, was still given a cupcake of her own that morning.

There is the way everyone else saw Alexis and then there was what happened that morning. Either she was punished for not doing her homework or she wasn't. There is no such thing as compromise when it comes to punishment. Punishment was always full and exacting in my mother's household. So, this was one of those things, one of many things in fact, that did not make sense on that particular day. I was taught that if something doesn't make sense, it's a lie.

Now to claim that Alexis ran away. What 7-year-old runs away? Where would she run to? How would she keep herself clothed or fed? Where would she sleep? I believe in my heart that my innocent child was the victim of foul play at the hands of those who have lied to cover up their negligence or their own selfish desire to rid themselves of a child they care nothing about.

As I sit here and write - painting you a picture of how sweet my daughter was - I reflect on the relationship we had and the effect she had on others. I also reminisce on the other incident I wish Alexis hadn't witnessed but one she brought me to laughter over.

Alexis had never seen me argue with or be disrespectful toward her mother. As for the incident that happened four years prior when she was 2, I'm fairly certain she did not remember. This time Alexis was three months shy of her 7th birthday. It was the beginning of 2002 and we were in the middle of a bad snowstorm. Alexis was the only child to come over on this particular weekend.

Special's mother and I, who I have six other children with, were having a heated argument. Wanting to avoid further verbal exchanges with her and not wanting to see the situation escalated any farther than it had, I decided to take Alexis with me over to my mother's house on 5th st. Alexis and I left and the roads were very slippery and visibility was near zero, so I was cautious as I proceeded. I was still upset over the argument I just had and I assume that Alexis could sense that I was out of sorts.

I was muttering to myself under my breath, so Alexis decides that she wants pizza. She said to me, "Daddy, I'm hungry, can we go to Rocky Ro-Co-Cos?" I said to her, "Alexis, that's on the East Side and it will take forever to get there in this weather." She replied, "Daddy, I know you're mad at my stepmom, so you need to take a ride anyway. So, since you are already driving, I'm going to ride with you and we can ride to Rocky

Ro-Co-Cos, right?" I just shook my head and said, "Baby, you something else." Then I began to laugh as we headed to the pizza restaurant. It was those kinds of memories that brought a smile to my face. I've only shared a few of those memories with you, the reader but there are so many others that I cherish that are too numerous to mention here.

As I write about how sweet, lovable and innocent Alexis is, it's so painful. Painful because I still do not have the answers to the many questions I still have. The whys, the what for and most of all - what more could I have done or can still do? It's not about anything else for me but answers, actions that still need to be taken and the reunification with my daughter. I don't wish this type of pain and turmoil on anyone for any reason.

This whole thing hasn't just taken its toll on me personally but physically also. I have gray hairs now because I worry constantly about Alexis. I have high blood pressure problems as a result of her disappearance and have experienced unexplained weight loss. Spiritually, I'm strong because of my faith in GOD but mentally I'm on an emotional roller coaster. My heart had a void in it because such an important part of it is missing.

I would like to thank all the people who helped assist the police in their investigation or me and my family in finding Alexis. I would also like to thank everyone who offered their prayers for Alexis and my family and still do to this day. Then there are the people who kept Alexis' disappearance relevant, including the media. And while I am Alexis' father, she is also the community's child.

– MAY GOD BLESS YOU ALL –

CHAPTER 3
ANIMOSITY

September 1996 is when I first knew that the number one suspect existed. One day I was at work on my lunch break and I called Alexis' mother to see how she was doing on pampers, baby wipes, milk, baby food and things of that nature. Alexis' mother's cousin answered the phone and told me to hold on. Several seconds went by before some guy got on the phone, asking me who I was all hyped up with a lot of attitude in his voice.

I said, "Who is this?" Then he said something vulgar that revealed to me that he was Alexis' mother's man. So, I said in reply to him, "So, put my baby mama on the phone!" When I said that it must have struck a nerve with him, because he became angry and started cussing me out.

I then replied, "Listen dog, I ain't calling to lip box with you, put my baby mama on the phone, mark!" He started to say something else disrespectful out of his smart-ass mouth but I just hung up on him.

About a week after that incident, my girl and my mother were taking Alexis home from spending the weekend with us. We were living in an apartment building on Port Washington Road that I mentioned in the previous chapter. That weekend was just like any other weekend, nothing out of the ordinary. I had my oldest daughter Diamond over that weekend as well as Randy, Zacary and Kadejah who are my nephews and niece. We had our usual wrestling matches even though Alexis and Special were only toddlers. I still took them to the park and afterward we ate and watched movies on cable until they fell asleep. Like I said, nothing out of the ordinary. Just spending quality time with each other.

I mentioned before that I always made an effort to have my children around each other as much as I could when I didn't have to work on the weekends. I wasn't selling drugs at this time because I had a good job working constructions and that allowed me to spend more time with my children. I was earning an honest living and not running around chasing money doing other things. Up until the time Alexis had to go back home, I hadn't thought about the stunt the number one suspect had pulled the week before on the phone.

However, I knew that I had to deal with the situation and make sure it never happens again. As my girl got Alexis and Diamond ready to go home, she said she needed to run some errands in addition to taking Alexis home. My mother said she would go with her because she needed to pick some things up from the store. I was relaxing and truthfully, I didn't feel like being an errand boy for the next few hours, so Special and I stayed home. After my girl and my mother returned home hours later, my girl told me that the number one suspect came out of the house when they dropped Alexis off yelling at them.

My girl had on my hat and coat so he mistook her for me. I jumped up with the intention of going over there to beat the crap out of that mark. I had never met this guy, didn't know what he looked like or anything and I didn't know what he had against me or why he was so bitter. But he was disrespecting me and now my girl as well. He needed to be checked royally despite the source of his behavior. My girl told me not to let my emotions get the best of me. She also reminded me not to disrespect Ms. Betty's house by going over there with the intent of kicking this guy's butt. She said it would be better if I would catch him in the streets and that would be a better time to take care of the business I had with him. And she didn't say it in those words. I did end up chilling out, but I was still mad about the situation.

Five days later, it was Friday and I had just left work. Alexis' mother called me and wanted me to keep Alexis while she and the number one suspect went up North of Milwaukee to OshKosh Wisconsin. I knew what she was up to because she told me and I respected the fact that she didn't want to expose our daughter to that lifestyle of dancing, stripping or any of the other lewd activities that fall into those categories. At the time I trusted her but looking back on things, I should have questioned whether or not the number one suspect should have been around Alexis. He had given me every reason to believe that he was up to no good and it was apparent that he didn't have the best interest of Alexis or her mother at heart. What type of man would allow someone he claims to love indulge in that kind of extracurricular activity and be okay with it? The people I grew up with played the field, we would sweat, bleed and cry for the money they earned and our significant others would take care of home, go to school or work if they wanted to. None of us were bums and we certainly didn't allow our women to put their freedom at risk for anything.

Alexis' mother and dude would be arriving in about 15 minutes to drop her off. I was anxious because I was finally going to see who this guy was that pulled all this nonsense with me. I put on my steel-toe boots and then went downstairs in the hallway, waiting for him to arrive. Alexis' mother's car came into view, I walked out of the building.

The number one suspect got out of the car and immediately started apologizing for his previous actions, saying that it was all a big misunderstanding. Alexis' mother came over to me and quickly placed Alexis in my arms like I couldn't have easily put her down if there were a physical altercation between myself and the number one suspect. But I didn't put Alexis down.

By the time the number one suspect made it to where I was, Alexis and her mother were standing and dude had his arm extended wanting to shake my hand. I didn't accept his offer and said, "Fuck, I don't even know you to have a misunderstanding with you but don't let that hoe ass shit happen again." Then I turned my back on him and Alexis and I walked into my apartment building. I knew then this guy did not want any sort of problems with me. He was just all talk and no action; and when I say he was all talk, I mean that literally as you will see for yourself before the end of this chapter.

As time went on, I didn't know what kind of seeds the number one suspect was planting in Alexis' mother's head that would make her lie about me to my girl. I was not sneaking around having sex with her when it came to my responsibility to Alexis. I would handle my own business regarding her care and her needs. And if I couldn't get what was needed for Alexis, my mother made sure it was taken care of; bless her heart. So, what kept running through my head was: why was Alexis' mother so bitter toward me? She and I have had misunderstandings but I didn't think it would drive her to be vindictive and tell my girl fabricated stories about me. She had a man of her own and the number one suspect and she had been together the same number of years as my girl and I had been together.

That brings me to an incident that happened in the winter of 1999. We were living on 42nd and Garfield, just seven blocks from where Alexis lived. We had the latest addition to our family, my gracious daughter Promise, born May 22, 1999, the second of our six children.

My girl was walking to the store when Alexis' mother began saying the same old bogus things about me again and the number one suspect spotted her. They pulled over and approached her. Alexis' mother began saying the same old bogus things about me again and the number one suspect joined in, co-signing all her statements. Now I had both of them conspiring against me and for what?

She even had the audacity to tell my girl that she could hook her up with her cousin.

Obviously the number one suspect had some kind of unique influence over Alexis' mother that I didn't fully appreciate or understand. However, it was beginning to trickle down into my household as the years went by. I'm not a 'messy' person as far as negative influences go in my life; even though this man was doing his best to undermine the rapport I had with my girl.

And despite not giving a damn about this guy, I never ran to him when they were married and told him that Alexis' mother had this other dude she was messing around with, bringing her to drop Alexis off and pick her up when I lived on 9th St. Nor did I mention the apartment the guy she was messing with got for her on 75th St., when they were having marital problems. The apartment he got her is so that the number one suspect couldn't find her. I didn't say anything about those things because it wasn't my business or place to say such things.

My instincts about the number one suspect were validated after Kenya Jr. was born on January 1, 2001. He was the third of the six children my girl and I had together. One of my friends, Vee, had told me that summer the number one suspect was in fact a snitch. I told Vee that I knew he was a mark but that a snitch was a very strong accusation to make against anyone without proof. Vee said that he had seen the number one suspect on the news in court testifying against a man named Booker. Then Vee went into specifics of the situation.

The number one suspect was the getaway driver for Booker when he robbed a bank on October 28, 1994 in the city of Glendale Wisconsin which is on the outskirts of Milwaukee. A police officer was killed during the robbery. Booker and the number one suspect had gotten away and the police had no clues. That is until the number one suspect caught a minor case unrelated to the bank robbery/homicide. He didn't want to do any prison time on the case he just caught, so he gave the police information on the unsolved bank robbery/homicide and told on Booker. The number one suspect agreed to testify against Booker in exchange for immunity. Hence, Booker was given a life sentence and the number one suspect was free to roam the street again. I asked Vee why he didn't tell me all this sooner. Vee was very truthful and accurate in his response. He told me that he didn't know who Alexis' mother was dating at the time. That is until Vee saw the number one suspect and Alexis' mother together on this particular day bringing Alexis over to my house. Then Vee remembered that he had seen the number one suspect on the news in 1995 and then told me what he did. 6 months after Vee told me about dude, I made a trip over to their house and beat him up. This time he wasn't going to run away like a coward nor will he be able to talk his way out of it either.

It was February 2002, about a week after the last time I saw my precious daughter Alexis. I recalled Alexis, her mother and the number one suspect who had driven down by me when I was at my mother's house. I had given Alexis $35, all in singles and placed it in her hands for a trip they were taking to a family affair in St. Louis.

The relative's house they went to stay at was next door to the rapper Nelly's aunt or mother. All I knew was that it was family of his. Anyway, Alexis' mother wanted me to give Alexis $100 but I told her, "What

6-year-old child is going to spend $100 in two days on candy and food?" So, I refused to give it to her.

This was a Friday and they were due back on Sunday. So, it wasn't difficult to conclude that Alexis' mother wanted the additional money for her and the number one suspect, not Alexis. Therefore, what I gave Alexis and placed in her hand, was enough for her and her alone. I remember a time when my mother had given Alexis' mother $100 because she was told that Alexis needed a few items like socks, t-shirts and panties. Sometime later, she called me herself and got mad at me, telling me that the money my mother intended for Alexis she gave to the number one suspect. I made sure that didn't happen this time.

After I gave Alexis the money, she kissed me and said, "I love you daddy." I told her, "I love you too baby." They pulled away and I saw her waving at me from the back seat of the car with a smile on her face. That was the last time I saw my angel. I cherish those last few moments we had together before she disappeared in May of 2002.

When they got back a couple of days later, Alexis' mother called my cell phone talking crazy on my voicemail. I attributed it to the fact that I didn't give Alexis the $100 like she wanted me to but on the voicemail, she was very disrespectful. But what really upset me was when she was talking about the children my girl and I had together. That was so petty on her part. Who does that? If she had a problem with me, which she shouldn't have, it should have stayed between the two of us. However, by lashing out the way she did, it brought everything to a whole new level.

When I heard her message, I immediately called her back with the intention of telling her a few things about herself but I was unable to reach her on her cellphone. I then called her house and the number one suspect answered the phone. He said she wasn't home. So, I asked him to talk to his wife about disrespecting my children. If she had a problem with me, then she should handle it with me and leave my children out of it. Then the number one suspect had the nerve to say to me, "Hell, I don't blame her." I snapped back at him, "Hoe ass mark, I tried to holla at you like a playa, but if you don't check yo' wife, I will and beat yo' ass if you want to defend her honor!"

He said something that made me take the phone away from my ear and look at it after he said it. I thought to myself that this fool can't be serious. He told me to meet him by his guy's house, this smooth brother named Dee that I also knew. Dee stayed two blocks and around the corner from me. I was living on 2nd and Nash at the time. After the number one suspect's tirade on the phone, I got back on the phone and said, "Bitch, you know where I stay. Come and see me! Better yet, I'm on my way to see you!" I hung up the phone, then my brother-in-law and I jumped in my Cadillac and went to their house.

When we got there, no one answered the door - big surprise. When I got a hold of the number one suspect on the phone several hours later. I asked him where he was when I came to his house. He told me that he went to Dee's house to meet up with me. I just called him a coward and hung up the phone on him. That was the last time I spoke to him until Alexis came up missing May 3, 2002.

CHAPTER 4

CONFUSION

March 6, 2002 was when K-Tre was born. He was the 4th child born to my girl and I. Unfortunately, the day we brought him home from the hospital I wound up going to jail just 30 minutes later for driving after revocation. A warrant had been issued for my arrest but not because the police knew I was driving after revocation, it had to do with an investigation that was ongoing; having to do with the dealing of drugs when I lived on 9th St. The detectives in charge of the investigation planned to raid my residence but I moved to 2nd and Nash before they were able to do so.

We were stopped at the traffic light on 8th and center when I saw the detective's unmarked police car in my rear-view mirror. I knew who they were because I had caught them watching me before with binoculars. When I lived on 9th St. A lesbian couple I used to supply came to see me one day and when I got in their truck to serve them their marijuana, they told me they had seen two detectives on the other block, facing my way looking through binoculars.

I wanted to see for myself, so I told the couple to go around my block and come into the alley behind my house. While they were doing that, I went into my house then out my back door, through my backyard and got into their truck once we reached the alley. Their truck had tinted windows so it was easy to do a drive-by to see if the detectives did indeed have his house under surveil- lance via binoculars. So, we drove to where the couple had seen the two detectives and sure enough, there they were looking at my house through binoculars. As we were about to drive past them, I told the driver to stop and she did alongside them. I rolled down the window and said to them,

"Y'all should be more inconspicuous." Then I rolled up the window, and we drove off.

Now on the day my newborn son was born, myself and my brother-in-law 'L' were on our way to deliver two ounces of marijuana to a buyer when we came to that stoplight on 8th and center; and I knew they were going to stop us. I saw the driver of the detective's vehicle put the cherry on top of their car before the light went green, so I said, "Bro, these po-po's 'bout to sweat our black ass' and I'm 'bout to go to jail." Then 'L' said, "Give me that weed because it's you they really want anyway. I'm clean." This meant that 'L' didn't have any warrants on him. So, I passed it to him and he put it in his drawers. As soon as the light turned green, they turned their siren with the lights flashing. I drove through the intersection, then pulled over to the side of the curb.

They both got out of their vehicle and then walked to either side of my car. One asked me for my license and the other asked my brother-in-law for his I.D. I didn't have my license so I was asked to step out of the car as was my brother-in-law. They checked us, then checked my car. Then they put me in their unmarked car and 'L' back in my car. They ran my name and his, then gave 'L' my keys and off to jail I went for driving after revocation and the warrant out on me.

Less than 60 days later, my whole world turned upside down. It was Saturday morning May 4, 2002 and my girl came to see me at the House of Correction. When the officer called my name for a visit, I was happy because it's always a good thing to be thought of when you're behind the walls.

However, when I walked up to the visiting booth, I knew something was wrong right away. My girl was crying and looking sad. I quickly sat down and picked up the visiting phone and said, "Baby, what's wrong?" Through the sniffles I heard her say that the baby is missing. I said, "What? Who's missing?!" My first thought was that we had a newborn baby a couple of days shy of two months. I thought she was talking about K-Tre as my heart was pounding out of my chest. She put her head down and said that the number one suspect had walked Alexis to school yesterday, but she never made it there. I replied, "What in the fuck do you mean she never made it?!" My girl answered, "Alexis never made it boy, and she's been all over the news. And the police are looking for her."

I was mortified, discombobulated and sad all at the same time. I asked how the number one suspect could walk her to school, but she never made it there. But the answers I was looking for my girl couldn't provide me with. After the visit, as I walked back to my dorm slowly, I broke down crying.

As I walked the hallway back toward the dorm, I passed a lieutenant and he said, "Sir, are you okay?" He wasn't aware of the disturbing news I had just received but he knew I was going through something painful the way I was crying. But I told him, "No" and kept on walking. He didn't push the issue with me but he did get on his walkie-talkie and followed me all the way back to my dorm.

People started asking me what's wrong because when I left for my visit, I was happy, talking, smiling and now they saw me dejected, distraught and crying when I returned. After I caught my composure, I told some of the guys who I interacted with that my daughter Alexis is missing, that she was walking to school by the number one suspect but never made it and that the police are looking for her. Actually, I didn't refer to Alexis' mother's so-called husband as the number one suspect at that time but there is no doubt in my mind that he is the number one suspect.

This was about 10:00 a.m. when I found out about the events of the previous day, so when it was noon, Alexis was the top story on the news. The headline was 'Missing 7-Year-Old.' Then I saw the number one suspect on camera saying that he hoped she ran away because she couldn't take some snacks to school due to punishment she received at home. I knew in my heart that Alexis wasn't a disobedient child and would never run away like the number one suspect had hoped. Besides, if he did walk Alexis to school as he claimed to have done, how could she run away from him? Certainly, he would have tried to stop her. He had to have watched Alexis enter the playground before he turned to leave. So, it would stand to reason that she would not have entered the school without someone inside seeing her and then waiting for the number one suspect to depart before leaving the school to run away on her own. What he said in front of the cameras was just something to appease the media - it wasn't the truth. And I also wondered why he had only a single tear fall from his eye while I went to my bed that night and cried like a baby. He wasn't cool like an upstanding man would be, he was cold as in cold-blooded.

Sometime later I had a conversation with Alexis' mother and she told me that she did whip Alexis' butt that morning for not doing her homework the night before. She also told me she didn't allow Alexis to take the cupcakes to school for her classmates, but the number one suspect put one in her book bag for Alexis herself. He told Alexis' mother, "Fuck that, that baby gonna take a treat for herself."

There was obviously a difference of opinion as to how to discipline Alexis in this matter but there is no logic in that. A parent shouldn't be checking as to whether or not a child does his or her homework the next morning. That's something that needs to be done the night before.

But before that conversation ever took place, when I had just received the news of Alexis' disappearance, it was more than I could bear. I cried so much in the dorm that night others couldn't sleep any more than I could. No one bothered me though, they all understood how much pain I was in and they tried to console me the best way they knew how.

The next day was the 5th of May and I was reading the newspaper about Alexis when I noticed at the end of the article that there was a police hot-line for callers to leave tips. I wanted more information concerning my Alexis, so I called the number collect and told them who I was. A police captain accepted my call and said that he would send a detective out to the House of Correction to talk to me.

An hour later I was called for a professional visit. I was escorted into a room where a Milwaukee police detective was sitting waiting for me. We went through all the formalities, what's your name, where do you live, height, weight, age, routine and so forth. Then he began to ask about the mothers of my children, where they lived, how many children we had together, their ages, etc. Then he surprised me with his next question when he asked me if I sold drugs and if I owed any outstanding drug debts. I told him that I did sell drugs but that I don't owe anyone anything as far as money was concerned. I even confided to him what I was purchasing. Three pounds of Marijuana for a little over $2000, but I also wondered why that was the first question he asked after the formalities were over with. He went straight to the subject of drugs without mentioning anything about the events surrounding the morning Alexis disappeared.

The detective did go in to ask me when it was that I had seen Alexis the last time. I told him it was about the 20th or the 21st of February. Then he asked me if I knew what type of guy the number one suspect was. I said, "Yeah, a snitch ass bitch! The detective also asked me if the number one suspect sold any drugs. I answered, "I don't know what that mark does besides get people life in prison."

Our visit lasted about an hour and a half, then I went back to the dorm. A sergeant was good enough to let me call home from master control in the annex building. I called my house and my sister told me that my girl and my mother were over at Alexis' mother's house so I had her call over there for me.

First, I spoke to my mother and then I asked her to put Alexis' mother on the phone. I guess she was so hysterical from what happened that the number one suspect got on the phone and told me she couldn't talk. So, I asked him what happened the morning Alexis went missing and he said that he walked her to school the day she disappeared and she didn't make it. He went on to say that they were doing everything they could to find her. I told him to find my baby, then I hung up the phone, returned to the dorm and cried some more. But if the number one suspect walked Alexis to school that morning, how could she have not made it? The only explanation would be that he didn't walk her all the way to school. As I mentioned earlier, Alexis didn't enter the school then run away without being observed, so the number one suspect must have stopped along the way and allowed Alexis to walk the rest of the way to school or they both stopped along the way and that's when she disappeared.

The next day was Monday the 6th and I had to go to court on a domestic dispute case. While I was in the judge's bullpen, some guys were talking about my daughter, her mother and the number one suspect. I sat there quietly and listened while they discussed what they thought happened.

The guy I was sitting next to was talking and said something to the effect of Alexis being the number one suspect's daughter. That's when I spoke up and said that I was Alexis' father. Then I pulled the newspaper article out of my pocket with Alexis' picture on it. The guy looked at the picture, then back at me and said, "Damn, she looks just like you." That's when the other guys sitting there expressed their sympathy and prayers for me.

Then that same guy and I began to talk. I won't use his real name; I'll just call him Hop. Hop was a member of the Young Gunz clique and he said that he knew the number one suspect and Alexis' mother personally. He also mentioned that he had a burn-out phone line in their house as we spoke.

Hop asked me if I knew of an incident that had happened at the house on 49th St. about a year ago involving a robbery. I told him that I knew of a burglary. Alexis' mother had called me one day and said that their home had been broken into and that she wanted me to keep Alexis for a few days. At the time I was on the freeway going to Racine, WI, so I told her to take Alexis to my mother's house and I'll pick her up from there. Hop shook his head, chuckled, then said, "No. Robbery!"

The Hop told me that he and his boys were the ones that did it. He went on to say that Alexis' mother's brother had set it up. Hop then explained how it all went down. Alexis' uncle was over at their house and witnessed the number one suspect get a quarter key of cocaine or knew where it was in the house. After Alexis, her mother and the number one suspect left that evening, Alexis' uncle called Hop. On the phone, Alexis' uncle revealed that there was nine ounces of cocaine at the house and for Hop to come over there to help stage a robbery.

Then they would split the cocaine in half. Once Hop and his guys arrived, they talked about how to pull off this caper without it falling back on Alexis' uncle. After they determined how they were going to do it, they kicked in the door, tied the uncle up to a chair but only gave him a quarter ounce of kilo of cocaine that was taken. I asked Hop why they played him out of his cut and he said that Alexis' uncle was a powder-head anyway and should be happy he got what he did. I was thinking to myself that instead of calling yourselves the Young Gunz, you should refer to yourselves as the Cut Throats.

Hop then asked me if I knew this short-mixed guy with long hair. I said that I did not know him personally. However, what I didn't tell Hop was that I knew the guy Alexis' mother had been messing with behind

71

the number one suspect's back when I stayed on 9th St. He would bring Alexis' mother over to drop Alexis off in a gold two-door Cutlass with gold Dayton rims sometimes.

Well, Hop told me that this was a friend of his and his name. He also mentioned that this guy and the number one suspect got into it over Alexis' mother. Hop told me other things that I won't elaborate on but based on what he told me, I was convinced that he knew the number one suspect and Alexis' mother personally and that he was being truthful in his conversation with me.

Hop and everyone in the bullpen thought the situation with Alexis had something to do with the number one suspect. Even before I told all of them who I was, some of the guys in the bullpen were saying that the number one suspect knew where Alexis was.

I finally got into court an hour or so later and my charges were dismissed. I made it back to the House of Correction early that afternoon and called my girl and sister to come pick me up since I was a street release. That meant I didn't have to wait until midnight to be released as long as I had someone to come and get me.

Now the House of Correction is in Franklin, WI only a 20–30-minute drive from Milwaukee. So, when an hour went by and they hadn't arrived to pick me up yet, I became concerned. I called home again and my other sister answered and told me that my girl and my sister had left an hour ago. Then after I got off the phone, I was told that I had a visit. With a frown on my face, I said, "Visit? Shit, it's time for me to be released!" but the correctional officer told me to take my belongings with me. That was peculiar in itself but of course I complied. As I was preparing to leave, a few individuals wanted my information so they could check up on me. That was love.

When I made it to the building where the visits were held, I wasn't led to a visiting booth but a room like before when I talked to the detective

48 hours earlier. When I walked in there were two detectives waiting for me this time.

The Milwaukee police department knew that I was about to be released from custody soon because my charges had been dismissed. So, they called the House of Correction and told them to detain me until they could come and pick me up. They wanted to question me downtown. My girl and my sister did arrive in a timely fashion to pick me up but were told that there was a disturbance in the institution and that's why my release was being held up. When the detectives made it to the House of Correction, they were told that I had family members waiting for me to be released. So, they went out to the parking lot, found my girl and my sister and told them they had to take me downtown for questioning.

Anyway, I walked into the room and asked the detective what was up. They said I have to go downtown to answer some questions. I told them that I had already spoken to a detective the day before. They told me that there were some additional questions they had. I said my ride was outside waiting on me. They said that they spoke to my family and they left. It was explained to me that my family would be waiting for me at home and that they would take me home after they were done questioning me. I instinctively turned around and put my hands behind my back so they could handcuff me but one of them said, "That won't be necessary Mr. Campbell."

When we got to police headquarters, one detective opened the trunk of the squad car to retrieve my belongings. I looked at him inquisitively and said, "why are you taking my stuff out if we are just about to talk, then y'all taking me home. Wouldn't it be easier just to leave it there?" Now I was beginning to feel uneasy about the situation but one of them said, "Somebody else might need the vehicle while you're being questioned and there aint no telling how long they'll be gone." I got the impression that the detective thought I was a dummy, so I said, "I thought you guys had assigned cars." At which point he put my stuff back in the trunk and slammed it closed. He simply said, "Let's just go sir."

We got into the elevator and went to a level in the municipal building where I was led to an interrogation room. It was a cold room where I spent an hour waiting before two different detectives walked in. They introduced themselves and took a seat across the table from me. The detective, who had a stern look on his face during the entire interrogation, reached into his suit pocket and pulled out a picture. He slid it over to me. It was a picture of Hop, the guy from the Young Gunz clique I had talked to earlier.

The detective who showed me the picture asked me if I knew the man. I said, "No, why?" The detective said, "Somebody that was in the bullpen with y'all today heard you guys talking. He is trying to get out of the time he's facing and said that you and your guy had a lengthy and deep conversation." Then the detective asked me what the conversation was about. This meant that they already knew what we talked about because this other guy had been eavesdropping on our conversation.

However, before I could respond there was a knock at the door. In came one of the detectives that drove me down to the police headquarters with my property in hand. He gave it to the older detective's partner, then closed the door and left. I just shook my head. Then the older detective said, "Now back to you and your guy." I told the detective that Hop wasn't my guy, even though I knew his full name and that I just met him that morning. I proceeded to tell the detectives some things but not everything we discussed. After a while they left the room and went a couple of doors down the hallway from me. I could hear chairs screeching around on the floor. Then it hit me, they had Hop in that other room.

45 minutes later they came back into the room where I was and that's when they revealed to me that I was a suspect in my daughter's disappearance until I was determined not to be one. I told them I had no problem with that since I had nothing to hide. I assured them that anything I could

do to help find Alexis I would do! I truly did not understand why I was a suspect in Alexis' disappearance since I was incarcerated at the time it happened. I paid child support, had joint custody of my baby and got to see her anytime I wished. It was dumbfounding to say the least but I accept the police department protocol in the matter. They had come and got me from the House of Correction a little after 5:00 p.m. and took me home around 11:00 p.m. that night.

In the days that followed all I kept hearing was that, "The media wants to talk to you. The media wants to see you." But I wasn't in any kind of shape mentally to deal with them. For the next two days family and friends came to my house to offer care, concern and empathy for me as well as Alexis. I didn't go over to her mother's house until the 8th of May but when I did, it was filled with people showing their love. When I saw Alexis' mother, I gave her a tight hug and held her in my arms for a minute. She was emo- tionally drained, so I kissed her on the forehead and whispered in her ear that she had to remain strong because we were going to find Alexis.

Upon entering the house, I received a lot of hugs from Alexis' mother's family. After interacting with them, I asked where the number one suspect was because I needed to talk with him. I was told he was outside. There was a large number of people in the front of the house. I would estimate at least 50 or more had gathered there. When I arrived at the house, I didn't see him around but I also entered through the side door of the house which was in the back. So, I walked through the living room to exit through the front door and out into the yard.

However, as I made my way to the front door, I noticed a video monitor on top of the TV. On the monitor I saw people on the porch outside. I went out on the porch looking for the camera but I didn't see one right away. The reason I didn't spot the camera was because it was up in the corner painted the same color as the porch. I thought that to be very odd.

From the porch I looked until I saw the number one suspect off to the side with a group of guys, talking on his cell phone. From the expression on his face, I could tell that whatever he was talking about on the phone was pretty serious. So, I walked up to him and said, "Say dog, let me holla at cha for a minute." He put his finger up and said, "Hold on playboy, this is important." Then he walked off in the other direction.

In the process of allowing the number one suspect to finish his phone conversation, I saw Alexis' uncle. I decided to go and ask him about the talk Hop and I had about him in the bull pen a couple of days prior before I went to court. I told him Hop's real name and asked if he knew Hop. Alexis' uncle said that he did know him and then asked what he said to me. I found that to be strange since I didn't mention that Hop and I talked at all. I just asked if he knew Hop. At that point I cut to the chase and told Alexis' uncle I knew about the burglary of Alexis' mother's house and that he set it up.

I said to him, "Remember when some people ran up in your sister's house and tied you up? Well, ole boy said he was the one that did it and that you called and told him what was in the house. He said you were the one who masterminded everything." Alexis' uncle got on the defensive quickly, saying, "I can't believe ole boy." I didn't believe him though.

Then Alexis' uncle changed the subject. He asked me if I had spoken to the media yet. I said no and he said before I do, I should talk to his girl. I'm thinking he's talking about some lady he's dating. Maybe she has something to tell me that I should know before I speak to anyone in the media. So, I agreed that I wouldn't talk to them until I spoke to her first. I walked off to try and talk to the number one suspect again, when I noticed Alexis' uncle having a conversation with a very attractive news reporter. What I didn't know at the time was that this was the lady he wanted me to talk to first before anyone else in the media.

It wasn't until later that I found out that Alexis' uncle had promised this news reporter an exclusive interview with me. She worked at Channel 58. I never watched Channel 58 news. I thought their news stories were weak. Alexis' uncle promised this reporter an interview with me in exchange for a dinner-date with the lady, which she agreed to. Actually, I think she would have agreed or said just about anything to be the first reporter to get an interview with me and the ratings that would go along with it. Alexis' uncle saw me when I arrived at the house and while I was inside, he was putting his scheme into effect.

When I made it back to where the number one suspect was, I pulled him aside and said, "Look man, whatever me and you had going on throughout the years, that shit is on the back burner. It's all about finding Alexis now." He said, "I'm wit' that."

Then I asked him what happened. He repeated the same story that he had walked Alexis to school that morning. I shook my head in confusion because I really didn't know what was going on.

Breaking the momentary silence between us, I asked him, "Hey, do you know Hop?" He said, "Naw." Then I went on to say that Hop said he knows him and his brother-in-law. He even told me certain things you have done. The number one suspect still insisted that he didn't know Hop. I didn't believe him any more than I believed Alexis' uncle when he denied what Hop told me. Then I switched gears on him, saying, "I don't think Alexis ran away." Before he could respond, one of his guys ran up and turned him around by grabbing his shoulder. His guy said, "come on man, we got to go, we got that call!" Then they ran off, jumped in a car and left.

While all this was going on, I noticed a reporter looking at me while I was talking to the number one suspect. It was not the same reporter Alexis' uncle had promised an exclusive interview to. This reporter was watching me from the time I began my conversation with the number one suspect until

I walked back inside the house after he left. Once back inside the house, I talked with Alexis' family members some more and found out that Alexis' mother had secluded herself in her bedroom from everyone.

A while later. I told Alexis' great grandmother, Ms. Betty, I was about to leave but first I was going to talk with the news reporters camped out in the front yard. When I was outside, I had seen them pacing back and forth hoping to get a comment or two from me. As I left the house, one reporter from Channel 6 walked up to me and asked if I was Alexis' biological father. I said that I was and then he inquired as to whether he could ask me a few questions. I agreed and the reporter turned and waved to someone. Before I knew it, every reporter from all the news stations that were there were headed my way. Microphones were in my face from all directions. The reporter from Channel 6 was closest to me. Then I happened to look to my left and I saw the reporter from Channel 58 standing with Alexis' uncle behind the Fox 6 reporter. The look she was giving him was priceless and it was almost as if she was saying to him, "You lied to me you piece of crap!"

Then the questions began. Question after question from different reporters, all trying to ask the most poignant question so as to better their competition. The reporter from Channel 58 did manage to ask her question as I answered the inquiries of all the reporters that were present. The questions I could answer I did and those I wasn't sure about, I left open to interpretation. After the questioning ended, that's when Alexis' uncle told me about his arrangement with the Channel 58 reporter. I told him that he should have referred to her as just a reporter and not his girl. If he had, he might have gotten what he wanted from her.

I went back over to Alexis' mother's house several days later after she and the number one suspect had taken lie detector tests. We were eating carryout food because no one was cooking during those days immediately following Alexis' disappearance. Then we saw breaking news come on the television.

Alexis' mother had passed her lie detector test but the number one suspect had failed his. The chump then knocked some things off the television, including that video monitor. He said the police were lying about him but I knew it was just a show he was putting on for appearances sake. Others were trying to calm him down but like he did when I tried talking to him days before, he jumped in a car and left the house on 49th St. but I did stay in touch with Alexis' mother.

The police wanted me to take a lie detector test shortly after Alexis' mother and the number one suspect did. I took the test a week later and passed it with flying colors. The results of which were on the news as well. In addition, the police wanted a DNA sample from me about a week later to make up a composite of Alexis' blood type and some other complicated things they were discussing. I complied with no problem and I didn't even mind when the police started coming to my house at 1, 2 and sometimes 3 in the morning waking me and my girl out of sound sleep saying they needed to search the house. They were searching the house, of all things, to see if Alexis was there.

Everything the police asked me for or about, I did. I don't care too much for the police as a whole but I knew my compliance would help find Alexis more than my defiance would. I was all about doing whatever it took to find my daughter - no questions asked!

Sometime in June, nearly two months after Alexis disappeared, I was in a place called Judy's Red Hots on Holton and Locust. I was with my sister's baby daddy 'L' and his guy, when my cousin's baby daddy, Corn, rode past the joint and noticed me inside. He proceeded to drive around the block and arrived back at the restaurant. Then he came in to talk to me.

He didn't know who I was with and wanted to speak to me alone. So, the two of us walked outside the restaurant.

Once outside, he asked me what I thought was going on with my daughter. I told him I really didn't know but I felt the number one suspect knew more than he was telling me. I just needed some proof before I jumped the gun. Then Corn said, "Listen, I don't fuck wit' dude but my brother do. Me and my brother were in their shop the other day when the number one suspect stepped to us trying to put us up on a robbery he was about to do."

Not even two months after Aexis disappeared, her mother and the number one suspect had opened their own store on the corner of 42nd St. and Bonny. They actually called the store, 'Alexis.' Needless to say, I was not happy about the situation. Here he is lying to me, lying to the police and now he has the audacity to open a store dedicated to my daughter. A little girl whose disappearance he probably had a hand in.

Later that day I was over at my mother's house when I spotted Alexis' mother driving down the street. I stopped her and told her what Corn had told me earlier about her husband. Now that I had her alone, I told her that she needed to let me know what happened the morning Alexis went missing. She told me about the homework and the cupcake situations and said, "He walked her to school." I said, "Are you sure? Because I heard he was supposed to meet somebody that morning about y'all opening y'all lil' store. And if he did, then he never came back to tell you that Alexis made it to school. How can you be sure?" Truth be told, Alexis used to walk to school with a little girl that lived a few houses down from her. The school was only about a 100ft or so from Alexis' house, plus there was a crossing guard at the corner. So why did the number one suspect decide to walk her to school at a time when he had a so-called 'business meeting' on the way there?

Especially when it was something he didn't ordinarily do. And where was Alexis' little friend she always walked to school with? Did the number one suspect and Alexis begin their walk to school before she met Alexis to walk to school with her? Was it after? Did this little girl witness anything that morning?

Even in news reports it was that the number one suspect left the house to go and meet an acquaintance that morning. It was about opening up the store they now had. The news reporters never mentioned the name of this acquaintance but I found out who he was the following year. I have always felt that this meeting was a major factor in this case. It's been so heart-wrenching to still be faced with all these unanswered questions even after all this time.

Despite knowing that the number one suspect had failed his lie detector test and all the suspicion surrounding his actions that morning, Alexis' mother said she believed her husband. She said that he would never do anything to put Alexis in harm's way. However, then she made a statement that was totally inconsistent with her belief that he would never hurt Alexis. She said that he was a killer and that she was going to ride with him! I could hardly believe what I was hearing. She was acting like I was the enemy. So, I had to try and bring her back to reality.

I said, "He's definitely not a killer but he is a squealer 'cause he squealed on Booker. And why in the fuck is he trying to do robberies when our daugh- ter is missing?" She continued to defend him, so I said, "Fuck it, then ride wit' the mark!" She drove away in a huff but I didn't care. I knew what I knew and now I knew something else – that Alexis' mother was defend- ing him. Maybe by choice, maybe out of fear but she defended him to me about what really happened the morning Alexis disappeared.

A short time later, a vigil was being held at Alexis' school. I wasn't sure what time it was being held at, so I called Alexis' mother to find out. But instead of her, the number one suspect got on the phone talking crap. He said, "Say homeboy, what did you tell my wife 'bout me?" I replied, "Mark ass trick, you're a snitch and a half-ass stick up artist." He started to talk tough but I knew that talk was all he was going to do so I hung up on him quickly.

I ended up calling my cousin Denett to find out what time the vigil was. I arrived at the vigil with my mother, my two little sisters and my guy Shawn. After the vigil was over, the number one suspect was looking at me with this crazed look on his face. I asked him if he had a problem with his face. He put on a little show in front of his guys like he was going to do some- thing but for all his loud talk and dramatics, he wasn't going to back any of it up. So, I told him that I was right here if he wanted to do something.

It was a little surprising to me that he chose to charge at me but that's what he did. I charged back at him. However, people got between us quickly and pulled us apart from all directions. Truth be told, I didn't want to get into it with him at my daughter's vigil but all the frustration I had toward him got the best of me. In fact, I was always planning on putting my hands on the chump when I got out of the House of Correction for all the crap, he was saying about me before I went to jail but when Alexis came up missing, my priorities changed.

Weeks went by like days and soon after the incident at the vigil, my auntie and her children went to live with my mother. One day my little cousin Shonda went to get her hair done at their store. Alexis' mother had a spot in their store where she did hair. While there, Shonda witnessed an inci- dent involving the number one suspect, so she called me and told me what had happened. I went there to pick her up and I hoped I would run into the number one suspect as well.

Shonda told me that he came into the store all hysterical with one of his guys. He told Alexis' mother that some guys were just shooting at him.

After telling her this he and his guy went back outside. 10 minutes later a teenage girl came into the store and tried to buy a blunt. Alexis' mother told the girl that they didn't sell tobacco products to minors. But the girl said, "well, that dude told me to come in and get one." Alexis' mother asked her which dude told her this and she said, "the dude sitting outside on that blue Cadillac." Alexis' mother went outside because she and the number one suspect owned a blue Cadillac. When she went outside, the scene she saw was inexplicable. There was a group of teenage girls around her husband as he sat on their car. She yelled at the girls to get away from him. One girl began yelling back at Alexis' mother and she spit a glob of mucus in the girl's face.

However, instead of defending his wife, the number one suspect told her to stop making a scene and to chill out. That's when Alexis' mother and the number one suspect got into a very disrespectful argument in front of the store. Everyone that was in the vicinity watched as he called her every name you could imagine. Alexis' mother didn't bite her tongue either. She replied with how much of a hoe ass bitch he was because his guy punched her in the mouth once and he did nothing about it. It was game on from there, he took her back inside their store and into the basement where they would see who the sole survivor would be.

When they finally emerged from the basement, the number one suspect was bleeding and it looked like his wife beat his butt like a seasoned veteran. Especially since she didn't appear to have a scratch on her. Alexis' mother once more got the best of him. It seemed apparent who wore the pants in that household.

Finally, the number one suspect left with his guy and that's when Shonda called me to come and pick her up. I was shocked and upset all at the same time. Here the number one suspect was supposed to be supportive of Alexis' mother in times of turmoil. Our daughter is missing but all he can find within himself to do is fight with her. He would rather add to

83

the turmoil by entertaining teenage girls outside his place of business and right in front of his wife. That raised a red flag with me and validated the suspicions I already had regarding the number one suspect.

I'll admit that in the beginning I was clueless, but as time went on and I gathered more information, I wasn't buying any of the story he was telling me. When I went to get my cousin, I saw the after effects of the one-sided brawl between the number one suspect and Alexis' mother. I also saw how upset Alexis' mother was. I asked her if she was alright and she said she was. I told her that she didn't need any extra stress because of him or anything else. Then Shonda and I left.

The last time I saw the number one suspect was at the vigil when he was putting on a show for anyone who was paying attention. This includes the news media who were also there. They were filming us at the time because I saw their cameras pointed in our direction. But they didn't show any of that footage on the news probably out of respect for everyone there who took part in the vigil.

In a bit of irony, it was just a few months later that he and Alexis' mother had to shut down the store because they didn't have the proper permit to operate a store. In the fall of 2002, sometime in October, I found out that the number one suspect ripped off a major dope dealer. I bumped into a friend of mine who I hadn't seen in years. She wanted to know what I had been up to but moreover she wanted to know how I was doing. I told her I was surviving and just trying to find out what happened to my baby.

During our conversation, Alexis' mother's name came up. I told her that she and that knucklehead, the number one suspect, had moved and I didn't know where. She told me that she knew where his homie's weed house was. This guy named E-Dub, who stayed in the same projects as I did when I was a teenager, operated the weed house in question.

When I was 17 and E-Dub was 24, he and his girl moved to Westlawn. I knew E-Dub well and he had even come by the house on 49th St. after Alexis disappeared. She told me where this weed house was on 12th and Burleigh, between Burleigh and Chambers, and gave me the address. After she and I talked, I went and picked up my cousin Wayne and went over to that residence.

I parked and we went and knocked on the front door. Someone from inside the house asked, "Who is it?" I ignored the question and asked for E-Dub. The voice replied by saying he wasn't there. As Wayne and I turned to leave, E-Dub pulled up. E-Dub parked his car and once we greeted each other, the conversation began.

During our conversation, E-Dub asked me, "Ken, what do you think is going on?" Referring to the number one suspect, I responded with, "I really don't know but the word on the streets is that he robbed somebody." E-Dub said to me, "See, people 'round here running their mouth and don't know what the fuck they talking about. Look here my dude, I introduced the number one suspect to my guy and one day my guy went to deal with the chump without me being present and the chump got him. But not knowing that what he got my guy for wasn't just my guys but me and my guys. So, in actuality, the mark owes me!" I asked him who his guy was and how much the number one suspect got him for.

E-Dub told me not to even trip about it because that's not important. Then I asked E-Dub if he knew where the number one suspect lived now. He told me no and that he hadn't spoken to him in a while because the police went to the store, he was operating at one time showing E-Dub's picture around and asking the number one suspect if he knew anything about him. The number one suspect didn't tell him about that, also because of his wife. I asked him what he meant by 'because of his wife.' E-Dub told me that the number one suspect was fucking off with other women but telling his wife that he was with him. So, his wife, Alexis' mother, didn't care for E-Dub that much and E-Dub didn't care for her either was what he told me.

Alexis' mother had been disrespecting E-Dub because she thought E-Dub was making the number one suspect do things he shouldn't have been doing. But the truth was that the number one suspect was his own worst enemy, creating his own problems. So, E-Dub stayed away from both of them since the number one suspect didn't seem to be able to control his wife's behavior.

Since he was revealing all the hard feelings between Alexis' mother and himself, I asked if he was the one who punched her in the face. E-Dub just laughed and never said whether he did or didn't do it. We talked a few more minutes before Wayne and I turned to leave. However, before we departed, E-Dub made it clear that he had zero tolerance having to do with what happened to Alexis. If the number one suspect and I went to war, E-Dub also made it clear that he would simply step aside and let me handle my business with him.

I ended up going back to the House of Correction for a driving ticket from 1997 that came up in 2003. The city of Milwaukee had hired several people to work in their traffic division who went through old files to see who had unresolved driving cases. While there this time I ran into Alexis' mother's cousin who I'll call J.G.

I didn't know J.G. but he knew me. He said, "Kenya, let me holla at cha." I was surprised when he called me by my first name because everyone, I know calls me Ken. That is with the exception of my mother and aunties. Anyway, he walked up to me with tears in his eyes and said, "I can't take it anymore." We began to converse and he revealed to me that he was a member of a drug circle that included E-Dub and the number one suspect. He told me that this one guy was the cash cow named Hamilton.

Hamilton supplied the circle and he was also the one the number one suspect went to meet the day Alexis disappeared about opening the store.

It was at this point that I realized that Hamilton was the one E-Dub was talking about in our conversation, he just wouldn't reveal his name to me. J.G. disclosed to me that he started to break into Hamilton's safe house for E-Dub and the number one suspect, in order to steal items and cocaine.

Then J.G. told me that E-Dub and the number one suspect had started partially paying for the cocaine Hamilton had fronted them. After a while, J.G. said that Hamilton was beginning to find himself in debt to his own people. He subsequently assumed that someone in his circle was stealing from him. The last straw for Hamilton was when he gave the number one suspect half a kilo of cocaine to hold but the number one suspect came up with the idea to fake a drug raid instead. He messed up the house to make it look as if the police raided it. Then he called Hamilton to come over to see for himself what happened. Hamilton did show up to see what happened but the thing about drug raids is that whenever the police conduct one, they always have a search warrant. They either present it to the occupants of the home or post it on the door if no one is home. This way no one can make the claim that they were never served. The number one suspect couldn't produce a copy of the search warrant and this raised Hamilton's suspicions about the number one suspect. J.G. told me that during the 60 days or so that I was incarcerated, the circle would meet at the house on 49th St. every morning snorting cocaine lines before they went out to sell drugs for that day.

After Alexis went missing, Hamilton stayed around until he got arrested in a drug sting a month and a half later on June 26, 2002. Prior to that, he would tell his circle to bring all the money they made on the sale of drugs to the house.

Hamilton told them not to worry because he would repay them but it was important to bring all the money they had because they were going to get a phone call about Alexis! Was this money a ransom payment for Alexis? These statements by Hamilton were all made after Alexis disappeared.

Upon my release from the House of Correction, J.G. and I had another conversation. He told me that he helped the number one suspect sell what was stolen from Hamilton under the pretense of a staged police raid. J.G said that he kept the cocaine under the doghouse in the backyard while the police were over at the house investigating Alexis' disappearance almost every day. There was also the media and a number of family members at the house on a constant basis day after day.

J.G. also said that he helped the number one suspect sell it at a low price of $10,500 dollars. I personally remember hearing of shopping sprees, honey-moons and vacations months after Alexis' disappearance that the number one suspect and Alexis' mother took together. J.G. said that Alexis' mother helped the number one suspect spend the money. He said that he couldn't stand to see me suffer any longer and wanted me to know the truth. This was Alexis' mother's cousin saying all this to me. He wasn't related to me, so I didn't see any reason why he would lie to me. I have to respect and admire him for his honesty.

After I served my 20-day commitment, I was released. On that day I was over at my sister's house and she was on the phone with her children's father, 'L', who was the one who was with me the day the detectives pulled us over. 'L' was in the Correctional Community Center, which was the Huber facility for the House of Correction. He told my sister to put me on the phone. 'L' said, "Bro, this dude wants to talk to you. He says he's Hamilton's nephew." I was instantly intrigued. I told 'L', "Put the kat on the phone." His name was Emell and his first words to me were, "What's up my guy?" I replied with, "What's up?" right back at him. Then Emell got straight to the point. He asked me if I knew where the number one suspect lived. I said I didn't know; he and Alexis' mother had moved off of 49th St months earlier. Emell said he was looking for the number one suspect because he owed $50,000 dollars to his uncle and that his uncle had to have that money. I told Emell that if I found out where the number one suspect was staying, I would pass the information his way. I also added that if he heard anything about Alexis, I'd appreciate it if he would do the same. That was it for conversation.

Shortly after that, Emell went AWOL from the Correctional Community Center. I passed the information on to the detectives working on Alexis' case because I felt it was of value to be investigated. When Emell was booked months later for going AWOL, he was sent to the House of Correction to finish his sentence. The detectives went out there to talk with him.

I was told later on by a detective how the interview went. When Emell walked into the interrogation room, he was caught off guard. One of the detectives asked him to take a seat, which he did and the other detective asked him if he knew why he was there. Emell said he didn't know why he was there. That's when one of the detectives said that they were here to talk to him about the conversation he had with me when he was at the Correctional Community Center. Then Emell said that his uncle told him not to talk about this case. Then Emell got up from the table and walked out.

A short time after bumping into J.G., I had found a way to get in contact with E-Dub because he was no longer at his place on 12th St. I wound up going to his girlfriend's sister' house. I left my number for E-Dub to call me A.S.A.P. He did so and 30 minutes later he came to see me.

I told E-Dub about the conversation I had with J.G. in the House of Correction. E-Dub claimed J.G. was lying to me. So, then I asked E-Dub why J.G. would have lied to me. What would J.G. have to gain by doing so? E-Dub said he didn't know but that he was lying to me nonetheless. I felt

J.G. was being truthful however, because he laid everything out for me. Not to mention the fact that he started crying during our conversation. E-Dub on the other hand, was being secretive. He was asking more questions than he was answering. It wasn't at all like our previous conversation.

Now that I had a lot more information than the first time E-Dub and I talked. I felt he was being manipulative the first time we spoke and now he was trying to do it again. So, I asked him if he knew where J.G. lived because we can go over there right now and get this whole thing straightened out. E-Dub replied that J.G. stayed somewhere off of 22nd St. or 23rd St. and Center. I told E-Dub that I needed to know the facts before I started bringing drama into someone's life. He told me that he understood that. We spoke for about 30 more minutes, then E-Dub left.

I went back inside my house where my homeboys were and we talked about what we were going to do as soon as we thought the Milwaukee Police Department wasn't following me any longer. My guy Meech, who was my childhood friend, even offered to buy a house to kidnap the number one suspect and take him to. Once there, he could find answers about what happened to Alexis by torturing him with the blow torches and then pouring rubbing alcohol and salt into his wounds. After he gave up the information, then he could be disposed of. Meech said that we could not leave him alive because he would most definitely go and tell the police what we did.

I knew the police were watching me in the beginning because they told me they would be keeping a close eye on me and the number one suspect. If something were to happen to him, the police would be coming to get me. By the same token, if something were to happen to me, the police would be quick to pick him up also. The police also said that they were aware of the animosity between us over the years.

One day in 2002, I was over at my friend Dee's house. Just seconds after I left his house, some detectives pulled up and asked Dee how and where he knew me from. Dee told them we were close friends from way back in the day and that his mother took us to the Circle City Classic in Indianapolis Indiana when I was a senior in high school in 1992. His mother also brought Dee to see me in the hospital both times I was shot. I went to see Dee when he got shot as well. Dee just gave the detectives a little bit of history as to some of the things he and I experienced as youngsters since they asked. I didn't think they were going to watch me closely for too long though. It was probably going to last until I was officially eliminated as a suspect in Alexis' disappearance.

In 2003, things began to fall apart between the number one suspect and Alexis' mother. They had another huge fight, only this time it became a highly publicized domestic violence case that the media covered. It was a public quote by Alexis' mother that the media covered. It was a public quote by Alexis' mother that caught my attention however. Referring to the number one suspect, she said, "He sells drugs, he uses drugs, he pimps women, he's abusive and he hasn't been supportive of me since Alexis has been missing!"

I was blown away by her statement. It was just a year earlier that she told me how much she loved him, how much of a so-called killer he was, how she believed in him and would ride with him and would ride with him. Now she has done an about-face and told the media what really went on between them. Was I the only one to notice the lie they were living? I used to see them on the news and on talk shows like Ricki Lake and Jenny Jones, holding hands, looking like they were supporting each other. However, the truth finally came out. This domestic dispute caused them to split up.

One day I went down Center St. looking for J.G. I drove northbound on 23rd St, then proceeded across Center St. toward Hadley, when I noticed a dice game going on in the middle of the block. I pulled up to the individuals shooting dice, all of whom looked to be young teenagers 13 to 17 years of age. I asked them, "Excuse me young playas, do any of y'all know my man J.G.?" They all looked my way with one of them reaching into his waistband. The one who reached into his waistband said, "Who you playa?!" With an attitude, I told him that I was Alexis Patterson's father and J.G. was her cousin. Then I told him that I needed to talk to him. That's when the Kid's whole demeanor changed and he told me to hold on for a minute. He then pulled out a cell phone and dialed a number. As soon as the person on the other end of the line answered, the kid said, "J.G. Alexis' daddy is over here looking for you." The kid listened for a second to what J.G. was saying to him, then he closed his phone and told me to go around the block to 24th St. to a bar that's on the corner. That was where I would find J.G. then the kid went back to the dice game. I thanked him and drove off.

I arrived at the bar and went inside. J.G. was in the back of the bar with a female companion. After we greeted each other, I said, "I needed to talk to him."

J.G. said, "Let's go outside, I don't want the whole bar to be ear-hustling during our conversation."

Once outside the bar, we stood on the corner and I said to him, "You know I went to talk to E-Dub and he said that you were lying." J.G. replied, "Kenya, what did you expect him to say? Dude just doesn't want you to know the business to protect his own ass?" I said, "His ass? For what?" J.G. said to me, "What was going on. Kats don't like individuals in their business and I'm sure he doesn't want no contact with the po-po's, seeing that he was in the streets at all."

Then I asked him, "If he knew where the number one suspect was. He told me that dude was in Texas with this snow bunny he began dating. I asked how he came to know that and J.G. said, "because he called him a few days ago from a different area code and phone number. I asked him if he still had that phone number but he did remember the area code and gave it to me.

J.G. went on to say that the number one suspect had been shot by this snow bunny's ex-boyfriend because they were fighting over her. He said that a man called Meatball had been looking after the girl while her boyfriend went to do some time in the House of Correction. However, Meatball had no place to house her, so he took her over to the number one suspect who wasn't involved with Alexis' mother anymore due to the domestic dispute between the two. Meatball had left her there for a couple of days and when he went to get her, she told him that she was with the number one suspect now.

Jumping ahead a few years, I became Meatball's cellmate in 2010 at the Milwaukee Secure Detention Facility. I asked him about the situation between him, the snow bunny and the number one suspect. Meatball validated J.G.'s story from the bar years earlier and another situation involving a guy called Kenny Fly and the number one suspect. More on that later on.

Now back to what happened right after J.G. and I talked outside the bar. When the conversation ended, I went home and opened the Wisconsin white pages. In there I found the area code for Texas that J.G. gave me. I was certain that J.G. was being truthful about what he knew.

In fall of 2003, I wrote a rap song about my daughter's disappearance and I got some airplay on WNOV-860 AM. I also did some rap shows in the city of Milwaukee and Northern Wisconsin, letting people know how I felt and what was going on. I started hustling again as well. I hadn't done anything along those lines since Alexis went missing. My part-time job was only good enough to keep up with my child support, not good enough to support me. Also, on June 5, 2003, my girl and I had another child, a daughter named Treasure. I had to support her and all my other children as well.

My contacts with the police were fewer and farther in between. They wanted all the information I had accumulated on the streets, but they gave me nothing in return. They milked me for all they could get out of me and would only say that they were following lead here or a lead there. Sometimes they would tell me that nothing new had come in at all. All of which I consider to be a load of crap since Alexis' case file was over 10 thousand pages long. So tips and leads were coming in, I just wasn't being told about them.

It seemed as though the police were simply placating me at times. They would call me when something aired on the news and act as if they were telling it to me for the first time. What they didn't know is that I heard everything the news media reported on Alexis. What they were doing made me very uncomfortable.

There was another time they made me feel that way which I will elaborate on now.

In 2002, I appeared on the Catherine Crier Show on cable network's Court Tv with Milwaukee police captain Brian O'keefe, to talk about Alexis' disappearance. The captain and I met up at the Milwaukee Area Technical College's broadcast building where the interview was to take place via satellite from New York. After we had our makeup applied, we were escorted to the studio set and seated. The crew gave us both ear pieces to wear and the producers in New York thanked us for our participation in the interview. Then we were informed that Ms. Crier would be joining us soon to begin the interview. The cameras positioned and we waited for the interview to proceed.

I really didn't want to do the interview at that time because I had pink eyes in both of my eyes. But this was about Alexis and I needed to put my own discomfort aside for her benefit. I was committed to doing anything to broaden the search for her. Then the captain did something that made me feel uncomfortable - just like I mentioned before. It was also perplexing to me because what happened occurred during the actual interview.

If a question was asked that captain O'Keefe did not feel comfortable having me answer, he would kick my foot under the table and then give me a funny look. As a viewer you wouldn't have noticed this due to the fact that O'Keefe was outside the view of the camera when he would do it.

When he did it the first time, I took it as if he didn't want me to answer because he would cut me off and answer the question his own way. Then he did it a second time during the interview, so I acted as if I had to reposition my chair to move my foot away from him. Then Ms. Crier asked me what I thought happened. I told her I didn't quite know and she would be better served asking the investigators working the case. After I said that, O'Keefe jumped back in and did some more talking. In fact, he talked more during the interview than I did.

When the interview concluded, I asked O'Keefe why he kept kicking my foot and giving me strange looks. He said that he didn't want me to say something that might hinder or compromise the investigation. I asked him, "Like what?" O'Keefe told me it could be something I heard that really didn't have a factual basis to it.

I don't remember when but sometime before or after I did that national interview Court Tv's Catherine Crier, the Nation of Islam appeared on the local news and announced that they were the official spokespersons for the family. Alexis' mother and the number one suspect stood beside them at the press conference. After that day, I did not see any of the representatives of the Nation of Islam – and I always wondered why.

CHAPTER 5
GETTING ONTO BUSINESS

In the late winter of 2003, my little brother Jay came to me and said that it was time to 'tuck the number one suspect into bed', which meant it was time to kill him. But I still didn't know where he lived. All I knew as far as his whereabouts were concerned was what J.G. told me months earlier about him being shot and winding up in Texas. Jay told me if the number one suspect had been shot, the police would have a report on it. So, I went to the police station on Lisbon and North Ave. in an attempt to obtain the number one suspect's address.

When I told the police officer behind the counter that I was looking for a shooting report on the number one suspect, he asked me to spell his last name. Hell' I didn't know how to spell his last name (Bourgeois). It was an uncommon name and French at that. So, I told him to look up Alexis' mother's maiden name and see if that would reveal her married name as well.

Bingo, it gave her married last name and once the officer entered the number one suspect's first name, it confirmed everything J.G. told me. I asked for a printout of the report but the officer told me he was unable to do that since it was an ongoing investigation but he did say that I could have a summary. The summary told what happened, where it happened and the perpetrator and victim's names. It also gave me the victim's home address which was 1920 West Fairmount. Someone named Brad shot at the number one suspect seven times, striking him once in the leg and of course the number one suspect pressed charge. I paid $0.50 for the two pages and was on my way.

The house on Fairmount was a duplex that was a couple of houses from the corner. The lower portion had a sun porch and a children's daycare center was being run out of it. The upper unit was where the number one suspect resided with the woman he was shot over. We staked out his house only at night due to the fact that the daycare was being run out of it during the day.

The nights we did watch, we sat for hours at a time discussing tactics like how we were going to get him to talk and how we should dispose of his remains when we were done. I had just started to do ecstasy and one night I was feeling like I was invincible. So, I jumped out of the car and ran to the side door off the driveway and rang the doorbell. My brother and his associate followed me to the door but no one answered.

The last time we staked out the house, I was again under the influence of ecstasy. I was growing frustrated that we were unable to catch the number one suspect coming or going from the house. As we were smoking weed, I suddenly jumped out of the car, picked up a brick off the ground and hurled it through the windshield of a blue Suburban that was parked in the back of the house. My brother quickly snatched me up and carried me back to the car where he threw me into the back seat. As we pulled away from the house, my brother and his associate began to scold me and school me on how out of order I was.

I said, "What the fuck y'all mean I'm out of order?" Jay's associate re- sponded, "Ken, that shit was idiotic and you're just giving the hoe ass chump a heads up that somebody is gunning at his ass." Then Jay reminded me that this Brad fellow was already in jail for shooting the number one suspect, so by doing what I did, I was letting him know that someone else was now coming for him. After the two of them finished giving me the business, I understood where they were coming from. Unfortunately, we never caught the number one suspect.

Several weeks later I got busted on a cocaine charge with Jay's associate, which was in February 2004, and I sat in the county jail on a $40,000 bail awaiting trial. What was disappointing to me is that my cousin Shannon, who produced the rap I made about Alexis and did shows with me, had set us up.

Now almost two years to the day Alexis disappeared, I was incarcerated and I started to discover things on my own in the police reports that the detectives wouldn't show me and by people I was running into. Of course, people in my pod knew who I was after a while. One day while I was having a conversation, he told me he wanted to show me something.

He left the table we were sitting at and went to his cell to get some paperwork. When he returned to the table, he handed me a report with the statements in it that I read. My heart skipped a beat when I read a portion of the report having to do with Alexis. It was a statement from a major player in the Ghetto Boy's clique who stated he knew where Alexis was buried and he wasn't going to tell anyone unless he got a significant deal from the district attorney's office.

Now let me back up a bit. Remember I said that I had a conversation in the judge's bullpen with Hop, a member of the Young Gunz? That was on May 6, 2002. I also mentioned that there were things we talked about I wouldn't reveal. Well, there was one thing that is relevant to Alexis' disappearance that I feel I should reveal at this time.

Hop had allowed me to read some transcripts of a wiretap the Feds put on a member of the Ghetto Boy's cell phone. In the recorded conversation, the Ghetto Boy dude was telling Hop that the Feds had just pulled him over and for Hop to hurry and get to their shop to remove the guns they had there. The Feds were on their way to the shop, which was a car wash, on 33rd St. and Center.

The ironic thing is that the Ghetto Boy member in those transcripts back then was the same guy I was reading about now in the police statement the guy from Chicago had let me read.

As I read the report, I became upset because all this time I believed Alexis was alive and I still do to this day. I would have to be shown otherwise to think differently. It was also baffling to me to read that a person would use my baby as a scapegoat for their own personal gain. Nevertheless, that's what I read. The guy that showed me the statement ended up going to court one morning and never came back to the pod. Later that night a deputy came and packed up his belongings. I was grateful for his empathy though. To be in the position he was in but to still enlighten me as to the information in that statement, says a lot about that man.

One time I was laying in my bed when this guy named West rolled up to my cell. He literally rolled up to it. He was confined to a wheelchair due to being shot when someone tried to rob him a few years earlier. West told me that they were having a discussion on 860- Am WNOV radio about my daughter. He asked if I wanted to listen to it on an extra Walkman radio he had. I anxiously said yes and he handed me the Walkman he had in his lap. When I put the headphones on, I heard the number one suspect talking so I listened closely.

Then, all of a sudden, the number one suspect started lying his butt off about me. He said Alexis hardly knew me and that I was a deadbeat dad. I became so irate with him because he was trying to make himself look good to the community by lying about me.

How in the world could I be considered to be a deadbeat dad? I spent as much time as I could with Alexis. Every weekend or at the very least, every other weekend. When Alexis was with me, I provided a family atmosphere for her. She was happy and well taken care of. On the financial side, I paid my child support on time and I was not in arrears. My love and my financial obligation to Alexis and her siblings always came first. Whenever Alexis' mother needed me to watch her, I never refused her. To me it was another opportunity to spend quality time with Alexis. I made sure that she knew my side of the family just like she know her mother's side. Alexis knew her aunties, her uncles, her grandma, her cousins, and her siblings.

The number one suspect had to be high on crack and out of his mind to make all those defamatory remarks about me. I got so mad as I was hearing all those things he was saying, that my blood pressure rose. I was trying to call the station to let them know the facts. I wanted to tell the number one suspect to stop slandering my name and remind him that everything was 'suspect' regarding him and his involvement in Alexis disappearance.

When the operator would say, "Please state your name," I would say, "Alexis Patterson's father, Kenya." But for some reason, the calls wouldn't go through despite repeated attempts.

I was so desperate to get on the radio that I went to the deputy and told him that they were talking about my daughter on the radio and I needed to call my family to let them know. I asked if I could use his phone in the interview room, which is where the staff did inmate classifications and where psychologists spoke with people privately. The deputy really didn't want me to use the phone because he would get in big trouble if he got caught letting me do that. However, being that Alexis was my daughter, he told me I had 2 minutes to call my family. I thanked him and then he opened the door for me to use the phone. First, I called my house and got no answer. Then I called my sister's house and got the same results. I couldn't call my mother's house because she had a new phone number that wasn't able to get until days later. Then I tried the radio station again but the line was busy. I guess that's why I was unable to get through earlier. Shortly afterward, the deputy came into the room and told me my time was up. I was mad as hell over not being able to get through but not so mad that I forgot to thank the deputy for his efforts on my behalf.

Then West rolled up on me and said, "Don't let that bullshit that dude said take you off yo' square Joe. Just chill cause I got something for you to help calm your nerves." He went to his cell, a couple of cells down from mine and came back with some orange-colored liquid in a cup. I thought it was orange juice or something and I told him that I didn't want any. West said, "This ain't OJ Joe, it's hootch." Now I had never had hootch before in my life and I had to admit it didn't taste bad. Although I was mad at the mo- ment, the hootch did what it was supposed and got me intoxicated.

West made hootch once a week from the orange juice and sugar from breakfast and the bread from our lunch or dinner meals. I drank the hootch several times while in the county jail to take my mind off the stress of the situation I was dealing with. The sad thing was that after sobering up I would feel the same way and still be going through the same issues I was before I drank it. Truth be told, I was just fooling myself.

Before I caught my drug case, I had filed a motion with the court to stop child support payments going to Alexis' mother until Alexis was found. I was working a legitimate job; Alexis was still missing and her mother was still collecting child support checks from me. I wasn't even thinking about stopping payments to her until she did something ignorant one day and called my boss. However, my boss did say to her that she was not to call again regarding me because it wasn't any of her business. I respected that and I wish more people in the world were like my boss. What I think helped more than anything was the reputation I had on the job. My persona and my deposition spoke volumes for me.

Anyway, when my boss told me that Alexis' mother had called spouting whatever nonsense she was putting out there, it hit me that I was still paying her child support even though Alexis wasn't around. So, I decided I had to put a stop to that. We were given a court date that was scheduled for June 2004, by which time I was already in the county jail on the drug charge. The day of the court date, I asked the deputy if the family court knew I was incarcerated in the county jail. He called over to the family court and they told him that I would be produced for court via a phone conference. 10 minutes later, the court commissioner called the pod and spoke to me over the phone. He read the motion I filed with the court to me and told me that he was granting it. Then he wished me luck in finding Alexis. I thanked him and the hearing was concluded.

In July, another guy from Chicago named Solo came to the pod I was housed in. He was facing home invasion/robbery charges from 10 years earlier. Solo told me that he had dropped a cigarette butt at the crime scene and that's how the police obtained his DNA. He said he was scott-free until the Milwaukee police detectives came and apprehended him from his place of work in Chicago and brought him back to Milwaukee.

Solo said this one guy from the Ghetto Boys clique, who was a main-man in that crew, had told on him. The interesting thing was that the guy Solo was talking about was related to the guy who gave the statement that said he knew the whereabouts of Alexis and where she was buried that I had already read.

Solo said that he wasn't associated with the Ghetto Boys but that he used to supply cocaine to them from Chicago. Every day he would say, "I'm going to kill that dude when I see him!" He said this in reference to the guy who snitched on him about his crime. Solo knew the dude was in the jail with us and what floor he was housed on. For the sake of the matter, I'll refer to him as J.R, which are his initials.

One day I went on a visit and the library is right next to the visiting booths. As I opened the door to my booth, Solo was coming out of the library. I saw him glance at my girl as he walked by and said, "Yeah, this is my queen." Then I sucked my teeth, then closed the door and sat down to enjoy my visit. After my visit, Solo complimented me by telling me my girl was beautiful and asked if she had any friends or sisters that were available. I told him that she didn't have many friends but she does have some gorgeous sisters. Solo asked me if I could hook him up with a pen-pal or maybe catch a visit. I responded with I'll see.

I was on the phone with my girl the following night when Solo walked up to me and asked what was up. I put my finger up indicating to him to hold on, then I said to my girl, "Baby, is Khiem there?" She said that she was, so I told my girl to let me talk to her for a second. When Khiem got on the phone, I explained what was up, then I let Solo talk to her for a minute. Then I got back on the phone and finished talking to my girl. When I got off the phone, I asked Solo if he was happy with the way the conversation went. He told me he was and Khiem was going to drop him a line soon. After that I went to my cell. By this time, I had a cellie named Erma and Erma told me what Solo was on. For some reason he didn't like Solo. I told him what the deal was between him and I, and he said, "Fuck that mark, it's something 'bout that kat that don't sit right with me anyway."

A week later I was on the phone with my girl and Solo walked up and asked me what was up with Khiem because he hadn't received a letter from her yet. So, I told my girl to put Khiem on the phone. When she got on the phone, I asked her if she had written Solo yet, and she said, "No, not yet." Then she asked me what he looked like. I said, "He is short and has dark skin." Then she asked me, "What's he like?" I replied, "shit, he seems cool to me. He is from Chicago though and he runs with those Ghetto Boys." Khiem then said, "Naw bro, I'm good. That's okay." I said, "What do you mean?" She said, "Them bitch ass dudes jumped me." I said to her, "Girl, quit playing," because I thought she was joking. She said, "For real bro, I had whipped the shit out of one of them lame ass dudes at a party because he was out of order and very disrespectful to me." Khiem ranted about that particular situation for another minute before she moved on.

Khiem continued to go on about her experience with the Ghetto Boys. She said, "then a week later, after I fucked dude up, I was at the barbecue in the park and he was there with his guys and they jumped me. You know that scar I got under my right eye?" I said, "Yeah." She said, "That's how I got it! So, I can't mess with dude."

Then I turned to Solo and told him what Khiem told me. He then asked me if he could talk to her real quick. There was only two minutes left on the call, so I told Khiem to tell my girl that I loved her and I'll see her at our visit tomorrow. I then gave Solo the phone while shaking my head. As I walked off, I heard Solo say that he was sorry that had happened to her but he lived in Chicago and he really didn't run with them.

When I went back to my cell, because the pod was shutting down for the night, my cellie told me that the pod worker whose name was Rick, had just told him that Solo was in for a home invasion/rape, not robbery. Rick knew what everyone was in for because the deputies would tell him. I couldn't believe my ears and this dude had the nerve to try and talk to my sister-in-law.

The next day I had my visit and it went well as usual. But before my girl left, I gave her Solo's real name again in case Khiem forgot it. I told her to have Khiem call down here to see what Solo was locked up for. When I called home that night, I spoke to Khiem briefly and she confirmed what my cellie had told me and what Rick had told him - home invasion/rape. I told her not to write Solo, although I assumed already that she was not. When I got off the phone with my girl, I went straight over to Solo and told him that my sister-in-law had called the jail to see what he

105

was charged with. She said, "I can't fuck with that, oh no!" Solo tried to explain to me that the house he invaded with some other guys involved a woman who was upset that they wouldn't bring back the items they took from her, so she told the police that she was raped. I told him that he seemed to have an answer for everything and I just stopped talking to him altogether.

Soon after that ordeal, something happened to me that put me on an emotional roller coaster. Rick and I were sitting in the dayroom having a conversation and he disclosed to me that the drugs he got caught with got him incarcerated in the county for almost a year prior to my arriving at the jail. Rick told me that he knew who I was when I came into the pod but he felt he had to observe me for a time before he was comfortable to reveal to me a situation involving the number one suspect and him.

Rick said that the number one suspect called him for some cocaine. So, he took it over to where the number one suspect was, at the house on 49th St. When he arrived, he saw Meatball, a known robber, who I bumped into at the Milwaukee Secure Detention Facility and a group of guys on the front porch all looking at him. Rick then called the number one suspect and told him to come outside the house but the number one suspect told him to get out of the truck he was in and come inside the house. Rick then told him that if he got out of his truck and the guys on the porch were to rob him, he was going to kill him because he called him over there. So, the number one suspect agreed to come outside. A few seconds later, the number one suspect called back and said that his guy told him that he was straight, because all he had was enough for was a quarter key and not the whole kilo that was requested.

As we continued to converse, breaking news appeared on the TV saying that the Milwaukee Police Department got a tip from a confidential informant who was in the county jail, that Alexis Patterson was buried down south Louisiana.

When I heard that, my heart skipped a beat and I lost my breath. I was having a hard time breathing. I felt light-headed and the deputy had to call the medical staff. I had a panic attack and my blood pressure rose skyward. It was rumored that the number one suspect had a family that lived there. But Alexis was not found to be at the location the authorities had searched. After that, I stayed in the county jail another two months before I was sent to prison and the week before I was sentenced, I was shipped to the House of Correction.

On August 31, 2004, I was sentenced to 6 years in the Wisconsin State Prison System. My initial confinement time was 2 years followed by 4 years on extended supervision. The plea agreement I signed was for 2 years in and 2 years on extended supervision but the judge gave me 2 additional years of extended supervision. I was upset because everyone was telling me that my judge was lenient. Yet he gave me two more years on paper than even the district attorney wanted. This was my first felony conviction and my first time going to prison. Where was the leniency at?

My sentencing judge's name was Judge Khan and two weeks before I was sentenced there was an article in the newspaper about him. The district attorney argued that Judge Khan was too lenient on people that came into his courtroom with certain cases-mainly drug cases. Apparently Judge Khan had a reputation for not going with the district attorney's sentencing recommendations. He would always give less time. So, since Judge Khan was getting some negative media attention, he decided to begin making examples of people who went before him. And as it turned out, I was one of those people. After I was sentenced, I was taken to be booked as a state prisoner.

I sat in booking for a few hours and was sent to the state pod right before the dinner was served. The state pod was where everyone who was housed there was awaiting transportation to state prison. Some left within a few days and others waited for weeks. But if you were there, your next stop was the Big House. After we ate the food they served, we had to go back to our cells to be locked in while the deputies took their lunch break. When we were able to come out of our cells again, I was seated at a table with two older guys who were having a conversation. One of them asked me how much time I had. I told him I got a couple of years, to which he replied, "Lil homie, that ain't shit. That time is going to fly by." By his response I knew this wasn't his first time in prison. Then he went back to his conversation with the other guy.

Then one of them mentioned J.R in their conversation. Then I interrupted and asked, "J.R? Where is he at?" The guy that brought him up in conversation said, "That's him over there on the phone." J.R was the one Solo had it in for and the cousin of the guy that made the statement I read. They were both members of the Ghetto Boys clique. I had never seen J.R before, so I didn't know what he looked like. One look at him, however and I couldn't help but wonder how Solo was ever going to take him on. This guy wasn't little like Solo and he didn't have guns where he was heading.

I'll never forget J. R's face - dark skin, wore glasses and big-ass pink lips. He was 5'11 but he had a husky build. Definitely looked as if he could take care of himself. I wanted to talk to him about the statement his cousin made but since he was on the phone, I decided that I would go back to my cell for a little while until he got off the phone. But I ended up falling asleep and around 4:00am I was awakened by a deputy telling me to pack up because I was going to the Milwaukee Secure Detention Facility on a layover until they could get me to Dodge Correctional Institution in Waupun, Wisconsin. I was distraught that I didn't get the chance to talk to J.R. Our meeting certainly would have been beneficial to me but another opportunity would present itself in the near future.

CHAPTER 6

DEAD END

I made it to Dodge Correctional Institution on September 2, 2004 and was subsequently fast-tracked, so I only spent three weeks thereafter in which I was transferred to Stanley Correctional Institution, about 5 ½ hours from Milwaukee.

While there, in February 2005, something happened that offended me and I was appalled at the power that be. This particular day I was called up to the M.O.S (Main Officer Station) building. Now there are only 3 things that can occur when someone is summoned to M.O.S: 1. is the obvious, that a person would be in trouble for receiving a conduct report and would be taken to the box (segregation) from there, 2. A person may have to sign some legal documentation, which can be good or bad news for them and 3. A person has some sort of professional visit, whether it be from a lawyer or some type of police agency. 9 times out of 10 a person is aware of which possibility applies to them when they are called to M.O.S because they know their case better than anyone else. Therefore, they would not only know what they are being called to M.O.S for but they would also have an expectation to be called to M.O.S beforehand as well. So, I was caught off guard when I was called to M.O.S because none of the 3 aforementioned possibilities applied to me. I was stunned when the C.O said that I was wanted at M.O.S. When I got there, I was told that I had a professional visit at which point I was led into a conference room. As I walked in, I saw detective Louis Johnson with another detective I didn't know. I had a rapport with detective Johnson because he was the lead on Alexis' case. But I soon realized that things changed within minutes of this particular meeting getting underway. Now I'm going to share how this short meeting went verbatim.

When I walked in, Johnson smiled at me and said, "Kenya, man how are you doing? It's been a while, so how are you holding up?" "I'm alright," I said. He extends his hand for me to shake it and I oblige. Johnson replied with, "This is my partner." For the purposes of what I'm describing, his name is irrelevant. However, I did shake his hand also. Johnson said, "Have a seat."

I sat down in one of the halfway cozy chairs at the table and was hoping to hear some good news about my baby Alexis. "First off," Johnson began, "I want you to know that we're doing everything that we can and we are still working to find your daughter." I felt some B.S coming but I continued to play along and said, "I appreciate that detective, Johnson." Then he pulled out some forms and began writing on them. "Take your coat off and relax, Kenya," Johnson said. I complied. Then out of nowhere he said, "Damn you getting big, what you got like 15 months left before your release?" I replied, "Something like that but can I get out early if they grant me this 75% motion that I'm eligible for this October." "I hope you get it," Johnson said, "But hey, is your mother still living in the same place?" I answered, "Naw." Then Johnson inquired, "Can I get her new address?" I told him what it was and then he asked, "What about your sister Nicole?" I said, "She's fine and thanks for asking." Johnson asked for her address again and said that all this information would be helpful. I gave him that address as well. "Please excuse me Kenya," Johnson said, "Because it's just procedure that I write all of this down and I want to have it in the right places." So, I asked him, "Why are you writing on forms anyway?" His response was, "Like I said, it's just a procedure." I gave him a look that said, "I ain't no fool." so I responded with, "Procedure!"

Those look like statement forms to me! "Then Johnson looked at his partner and then back at me, then said, "Kenya, do you know what we're here for?" I answered, "To talk about Alexis, you still work her case, don't you?" Johnson replied, "Not anymore Kenya. Like I said, my colleagues are working hard on her case. I got moved to a different department and

I'm here to talk with you about a little situation that your brother was involved in."

By this time my brother was in custody for murdering a man in the late winter of 2003. This was by no means a little situation. That was a pure understatement. My brother's victim was choked out, shot with acid from a syringe, his head and hands were amputated, the body was set on fire and then dumped in a secluded area in Gurnee, Illinois. A year later a woman named Jennifer Z. Garcia, who was the one who drove my brother and his co-defendant to the dump site, got mad about a situation that didn't go her way and squealed to the Milwaukee Police Department about the murder.

I told Johnson, "I don't know nothin 'bout that!" Johnson then said, "Listen Kenya, your name came up and the D.A sent us up here to take a statement from you to compare notes and rule you out as a suspect. That's all." I told him, "Then go back and tell the D.A that I don't know shit!" But Johnson said, "Look, we got a statement saying you were involved and that you did this and that." He did have a statement in front of him, then he showed it to me. However, the person that gave it was lying because he was trying to get out of a drug case he caught. His name was Arthel X. Roders.

"Look, you don't have any proof or no D.N.A linking me to nothing! This is some bullshit, matter of fact, I'm done! Now let me out this Bitch!" I used my outside voice and called for the lieutenant as I stood up putting my coat back on. I assumed the door was locked because the lieutenant had closed it behind me when I first entered the room. As I walked toward the door, Detective Johnson jumped up from around the table and grabbed my arm. "Kenya," he said, "Don't do this man, please have a seat.

Let me talk to you." But I responded, "Man, get yo' fuckin' dick beaters off of me!" I jerked my arm from his grip, then the lieutenant came busting through the door asking what was going on. He told me to calm down because I was ranting on and on.

I told the lieutenant that I wanted to go back to my unit and he stepped aside to let me pass. I heard him say to detective Johnson and his partner, "Well, gentleman, I guess that this interview is over." My stay at Stanley Correctional was short, only lasting nine months. I arrived there the last week of September 2004 and left in June of 2005.

I was blessed to go to work release in Madison, Wisconsin but unfortunately, I had an altercation with a civilian at work which resulted in my losing the job I had at Willow Foods. It's a company that makes pizzas in Beaver Dame, Wisconsin. I went to the box for the altercation on August 30th and I was released on October 5th. I was then transferred to Columbia Correctional Institution, still maintaining my minimum status. Columbia Correctional was the penitentiary where one of my childhood acquaintances, Chris, killed the serial Killer Jeffery Dahmer, who murdered close to 20 people in Milwaukee, Minnesota and Ohio. Also, Jessie Anderson, who made headlines across the state for killing his wife at T.G.I.F's restaurant. Then he lied about it and claimed a young black teenager stabbed him and his wife.

Shortly after my arrival at Columbia, my cousin Trale came and was placed in the same barracks that I was housed in. As soon as he unpacked, we sat and talked when he told me that he was told that the number one suspect owed 25 racks to this dude named Doe who was the nephew of this guy that had been indicted with Jerry Walker, as well as our cousin Terrell, back in 1997. Trale said he had to let me know so we could investigate and get down to the bottom of this situation. I told my cousin that he wasn't wrong and that something was going to shake.

Just about 10 days later, this guy named Cooda came to our barracks and told me he knew Doe and all the homies in the 27th St. area where the ole 2-7 street gang used to cause havoc. I let Cooda unpack and get comfortable, then I went over to him to inquire about what Trale had told me.

When I got to his bunk he was chilling and watching something on the TV. I thumped on his bed rail and he looked over his shoulder back at me. He took off his headphones then I asked him if he knew Doe. Cooda looked at me inquisitively and his face frowned. I then said, "I'm Alexis' father and I heard the number one suspect owed yo' entourage some loot. I was just wondering if you heard the same thing, no disrespect to you." Cooda jumped down from his bunk because he was in the top bed and extended his hand for me to shake, which we did. Then he said, "I'm Cooda." I told him, "I'm Ken." Cooda said, "Fam, I don't know anything about that, but I just left the county jail and me and J.R were on the state pod and I'll tell you what he told me."

Cooda told me that he was having a conversation with another convict through the door that divided the two pods. He was asking the guy why he was giving JR some change on a lawyer if he knew JR was telling on him. The dude responded by telling Cooda that he was never coming home and that JR had a fighting chance. Dude told Cooda that he held no ill-will or hard feelings about the situation. Cooda said that he ended the conversation, then went to the table to go talk with JR.

At the table during the conversation with JR, he told Cooda, "Man, I'm finna go home." And Cooda asked him, "How?" Cooda told me he then said, "Alexis Patterson." Cooda then asked him, "Tell me something man, is she still alive?" To which JR shook his head no. Cooda told me that he tried to engage a little more about Alexis, but JR told him that he wasn't going to talk about it anymore. Then he got up and detoured to his cell. I thanked Cooda for the information and then went back to my bunk after he told me that. It was JR who had sent the police down to Louisiana in

2004, looking for Alexis' body. JR was protecting his identity when the police referred to him as a "jailhouse informant."

In early 2006, word spread throughout the joint that JR had arrived in the compound. I went to the library one day because a guy I went to middle school with and dated his cousin, worked there. I asked him if it was true that JR was at Columbia and he told me that he was. So, I asked him to look at the locator sheet and give me his name and institution number, which he did with no problem. This was the opportunity I had mentioned a little while ago that presented itself again. Going off of what I read about his cousin's statement and conversation I had with Cooda, I wrote him a letter telling him that he knew everything that went on in Milwaukee. I asked him if he knew the whereabouts of my daughter or if he could point me in the right direction to bring her home.

After I wrote the short but to the point letter, I dropped it in the mailbox. A week had gone by when I received a letter from a company based out of Menomonee Falls, Wisconsin. When I opened the letter, it read: Dear Mr. Campbell, Mr. Rhodes (JR) would like you to know that there are rules and etiquettes in everything that we do. Furthermore, he wants you to know that he has no knowledge of issues you addressed in your letter. Sincerely yours, Shonda Ford. After I read the letter I went and showed it to Cooda. He said that I must have spooked JR and being the intelligent individual that he is, that's why he chose to write me back via a third party.

One day I was coming from the doctor's office, which is up by the receiving unit (R & O) where JR was housed. As I walked past the picture framed window outside, JR's unit was exiting their wing. I noticed him, so I started pounding on the glass to get his attention which I accomplished. I pointed to myself then at him, to let him know it was me, Alexis' father. He pointed to a white dude that was in front of him and I shook my head no pointing back at him. JR then tapped the white dude on his

116

shoulder and pointed at me. I just shook my head, waved my hands as if to say, "to hell with this," and continued back to the barracks.

I had started writing a portion of this memoir while I was at Columbia and reached out to individuals in the media world to ask them if they would be willing to help in expanding the search for Alexis. I wrote Oprah Winfrey, then John Walsh because his show, America's Most Wanted, had aired Alexis' story. I wrote to black authors such as Vickie Stringer, Nikki Turner and Terri Woods. Of those authors I wrote, Terri Woods was the only one to show some love as well as interest in my letter. I truly appreciated the fact that Ms. Woods took the time to reply back to me. God bless her beloved soul!

A month and a half prior to my release from Columbia, two little boys from Milwaukee named Quadrevion Henning and Purvis Parker II mysteriously came up missing March 19, 2006. It was just like the way my precious Alexis disappeared in May of 2002. And just like everybody pointed the finger at the number one suspect during the investigation into Alexis' disappearance, so too the community pointed the finger at Purvis Parker II's father, Purvis senior. Purvis senior and his guys were the ones I was shooting off of the city bus in October 1992. Then I met Alexis' mother while serving time for that incident.

It's like the same scenario where drugs and snitching are involved. I had heard some unpleasant things about Purvis senior and although we had drama back when we were older teenagers, I wouldn't wish anything of that magnitude on him. I prayed for him as well as Quadrevion's family, for the safe return of the children. Truthfully, I didn't know if his actions played a part in his son's disappearance and that of his son's friend, but the streets were talking and when they did everybody listened.

Shortly after the media blitz and all the community gossip having to do with the disappearance of the two boys subsided, their bodies were found in the McGovern Park Lagoon on Friday night April 14, 2006. The Milwaukee County Medical Examiner stated that there were no signs of foul play and "speculated" that Purvis Parker II was drowning and Quadrevion Henning jumped in the water to help his friend but drowned during the rescue attempt. So here are two questions I have: 1. How did the medical examiner know which one of the boys went into the water first if their bodies were found floating in the lake a month after they went missing? 2. And why didn't they find the boys in that small body of water after searching it on three different occasions? Especially, considering that the last time they searched the lake they did so with a machine designed to detect human remains.

Now allow me to break down the meaning of the word "Speculate;" the word the medical examiner used. Speculate: to think or theorize about something in which evidence is too slight for certainty to be reached. Even though the families got closure, I prayed for a better outcome in their time of turmoil - like the boys being found alive. That situation saddened me because I was still going through the emotions of not knowing the whereabouts of Alexis.

Once I got released in May of 2006, my P.O locked me up in the Milwaukee Secure Detention Facility because of some rules I violated five months later in October. Now I hadn't seen Purvis senior since that incident back in 1992, which was 14 years earlier. When we saw each other, we spoke and we hugged. I gave him my condolences and he gave me his. I told him I was shooting at his guy that day because he was the one who exposed a gun to me and that you just happened to be with him. Purvis said to me, "Ken, that's water under the bridge. We are men now." We hugged one more time and told each other to keep our heads up. Then I went my way and he went to do his program.

Nothing really came about over the years about Alexis until I went back to prison in 2011 and ran across a letter. In late 2010, I was being revoked over some false allegations and as God as my witness, he knows I didn't do what was said. I didn't have a criminal case, just some untrue things my P.O claimed somebody told her and she decided to send me back to prison. She used the kangaroo court system of the Wisconsin D.O.C, better known as a revocation hearing to put me there. While fighting the revocation, Meatball became my cellie at the Milwaukee Secure Detention Facility. One night, while we were talking, he told me about a situation involving Kenny Fly, a major dough boy who got indicted and went to jail several years later. Meatball told me that the number one suspect used to get fronted some work from Fly and one time news got back to him that the number one suspect was trying to set him up for robbery.

Meatball, the number one suspect and some more guys were over at a house in the backyard, when Fly came speeding through the alley and to a screeching halt. He jumped out of the car with a duffle bag full of money and threw it on the hood of the car. He said to the number one suspect, "Fake ass trick, you suppose to be robbing me. Well, here's a phat bag full of cheddar (money). Now come and take the shit if you are bad enough, mark!" Meatball said that the number one suspect denied saying that and tried to calm Fly down who was already disrespecting him. After Fly saw that the number one suspect wasn't going to do anything, he picked the bag up off the hood of his car, threw it inside and drove off. Meatball also told me that Fly used to buy work from Demetrius Flenory a.k.a Big Meech from Detroit. I believed that because my homeboy's brother used to buy from Big Meech as well. And when I say "work" I mean drugs. My guy told me that Big Meech had come to talk to his brother one day in a cocaine white Bentley and as Big Meech walked past him to go into the house, he told my homie to watch his car for him. He made this request despite the fact that there were hoodlums in the car already.

Now, if you have ever seen the Black Mafia DVD, you would have seen Big Meech showing love and giving shoutouts to different cities across the globe and Milwaukee. Big Meech was definitely on the map. He also acknowledged Milwaukee again toward the end of his autobiography.

Well, I ended up losing my revocation hearing and I was sent to Redgranite Correctional Institution in February of 2011. When I made it to the receiving unit this brother named J-Rock recognized me as Alexis' father and told me that he wanted me to see this letter his cousin Jesse wrote. The only thing about this letter was that it was on another unit and in a different building at the time.

However, J-Rock did say he would get it from his guy who had it. Every few days I would ask him if he had gotten a hold of the letter yet and his response would always be, "Not yet. But you better believe that I'm working on it." Three weeks later I was transferred to a general population unit. The unit was E-East which happened to be the unit J-Rock's guy was on with the letter I desperately needed to get a hold of.

A guy by the name of Lil Gee (may he rest in peace) was the one who had the letter. When I finally made contact with him and read the letter, so many emotions went through my mind that I was traumatized for a brief moment. When I came to my senses, I asked Lil Gee if I could make a duplicate of it and he said that I could. Jesse was coaching his guy on what to say because he was going to have the Feds come and talk to him about Alexis.

The letter went like this: Fam-o, Remember when I was head of security for that brother Kenny Fly in the summer of 2006 and we used to ride down to Ohio weekly to get 80 kilos of cocaine? And we went to this house and you asked me who that little girl sitting there on the couch? I said, "Don't even trip fam, that's our mil' ticket!" Listen, don't look at it as being a snitch, just look at it as us reuniting a little girl back with her mother and family, you feel me? I love you like a brother and we grew up together so I'll do anything to try and get you out of the jam you are in. You're facing a lot of time and I'm here for you - and that's real talk. Then Jesse went on to give his comrade what he was writing, which was all of his contact information. He gave him his mother's address and phone number, his grandmother's information who lived out of state and one other address and phone number.

I believed the contents of that letter but there was one thing that wasn't true. The FBI agent that was named in the letter wasn't an agent at all but was actually, the new lead detective on Alexis' case. The previous lead detective, Louis Johnson was transferred to the homicide division. John Ressman and I had a good rapport together and he's the one that came and took a DNA sample from me in 2009 when some questions arose about some human remains found in Texas. The Milwaukee Police Department needed to make up a composite and perform other forensic medical procedures in order to compare the bone fragments found in Texas with what they knew about Alexis. However, nothing ever came from that discovery.

So, I made a copy of the letter for my own personal records and motives and I sent a copy to the Milwaukee detectives also. This way they could go to Ohio and open an investigation like they did in Louisiana years before, then in Texas years later. I also put in big bold letters not to leave out questioning the dude Jesse and his guy.

In 2012 my freedom was granted but unbeknownst to me, a detective was administering the investigation into my daughter's case, Erik Villarreal. I thought that every detective that was assigned to Alexis' case up until 2012 worked hard and had my best interest at hand, as well as the utmost concern for Alexis also. Now I believe a lot of personnel in the Milwaukee Police Department were sincere in their efforts and worked tirelessly to find Alexis. I appreciate and respect them for that and they have my undying gratitude, but this is what I'm troubled by. The lead detective, Erik Villareal, was praised by the family of a slain 5-year-old Laylah Peterson in 2016 for his work in helping bring her killers to justice. Laylah's homicide occurred on November 6, 2014 when a group of guys shot up her grandparent's home in retaliation. But they targeted the wrong house and wound up taking a precious little angel from her loved ones. I'm happy that Laylah's family received answers as well as justice. Now allow me to explain the conundrum I have with detective Villarreal regarding justice. Justice being the operative word.

Like I said before, I was back in the world in the summer of 2012 and 'L' was locked up again and was in the Chippewa Valley Correctional Facility. He was there with the number one suspect who was doing time on a drug offense. 'L' said to me that the number one suspect told him that he wanted to talk to me. I asked 'L' if the dude was around and 'L' stated he wasn't. After my conversation with 'L' I contacted detective Villarreal and said to him, "Check this out, I just got word that the number one suspect wants to talk to me. Why don't you wire me up and let me attain some information to help y'all out in my baby's investigation.

Dude never cooperated with you guys in the past or even spoke with me hardly ever. Maybe, he's finally growing a conscience and is feeling guilty about something and he wants to confide in me about what he knows." Detective Villarreal assured me that he would run it by his supervisor and get back to me in a couple of days.

After a few weeks of anxiously waiting on a decision and a phone call, my mother and I went to pay detective Villarreal a personal visit. When we entered the sensitive crime section of the Milwaukee Police Municipal Building, detective Villarreal greeted us as we walked into a room that held about six desks. Looking out of the window you could see the city of Milwaukee for miles because of how high up we were. On one of the walls, they had pictures of people that were murdered whose cases were unsolved and still open, as well as some missing people that were grown. As I was looking at the photos of the victims, I started to feel empathy for their families. That's when detective Villarreal said to me, "Do you see that file cabinet over there in the corner?" I turned in the direction he pointed to and acknowledged a gray cabinet that was about 5ft high with five drawers. He said, "That file cabinet is about your daughter and it's like 10,000 pages long." Now that I think about it, I feel that he was try- ing to butter me up before giving me the news that would possibly leave me discombobulated.

On that visit I was informed that his supervisor refused my request to wear a wire on the number one suspect who was the last person known to have seen and been around Alexis. I was baffled, insulted, mad and perplexed by this all at the same time. To keep my mind sharp regarding these kinds of things I watch shows like Cold Case Files, Forensic Files, Dateline NBC, 48hrs, Murder Mysteries and others. I watch those shows all the time and I've noticed that they have people wear wires on a regular basis to try and solve cases. What is the difference between those cases and my daughter's case? I expressed this sentiment to detective Villarreal and his response was that his supervisor didn't know what I was capable of and thought that it wouldn't be a good idea for the number one suspect and I to talk. Villarreal also said that since he was incarcerated, his supervisor wondered where they would talk. Detective Villarreal also added, "Plus, you're not on his visiting list." He was steadily feeding me these excuses, so I finally said, "Look man, (with a ton of bass in my voice) I ain't on no bullshit and I would never do anything to jeopardize finding my number one priority - my baby Alexis. Listen detective, this mark never wanted to talk before and now he wants to. That has to count for something. And far as where we would talk, dude is on work release (by this time he had gotten transferred to Marshall E. Sherrer work release center and obtained a job working in the community), put me in the area of where he's working at like on the humbug tip or at his job on the pretense that I just started working there. Shit, you guys are supposed to be the master manipulators and I'm sure that y'all can come up with a plan." I finally exhaled and waited briefly for his response.

Unfortunately, the end result was that somebody in the Milwaukee Police Department made the decision that I wouldn't be allowed to wear a wire on the last person known to have been with my daughter.

What was so sad about the whole thing was that my brother's co-defendant baby mama wore a wire on her man in May or June of 2006, on a visit to uncover information on a drug investigation. The entire situation had me confused and mortified, along with all sorts of other uneasy feelings. Detective Villarreal testified that he knew Ms. MacAfee wore a wire on Earnest Jackson (my brother's co-defendant). Now I wonder who allowed that? I found out about this occurrence in 2016. I feel that detective Villarreal didn't go to bat for Alexis the way he should have when it came to his supervisor in the Milwaukee Police Department. Especially since his supervisor was receptive in allowing a wire to be worn in a mere drug investigation and didn't avail himself to use that same resource and allow me to wear a wire in the far more serious matter - that of finding my missing angel. She was allegedly kidnapped for drug money that her mother's husband, the number one suspect, owed!

On Wednesday December 28, 2016, the Milwaukee Journal Sentinel ran an article on precious little Laylah Petersen again. This time it described how the case was really solved. Detective Villarreal and detective Kathy Spano were asked by their supervisors to take a fresh look at the case. During this time a guy by the name of Antoine Buchanan had called the detectives with some information about Laylah's case. Detective Spano was quoted as saying, "I believed him and that doesn't always happen." Buchanan offered to wear a wire on Divonte Forbes, one of the individuals who was involved. His request was approved and Buchanan was sent to the House of Correction to obtain recorded conversations. Buchanan was facing domestic violence charges, so him being there wouldn't raise any suspicion. Detective Spano also was quoted as saying, "We had to keep everyone in the dark except for a certain couple of people in order to make it successful."

Buchanan wore the wire for a week around the 4th of July 2015. The recording was non-stop and every day he had to be separate from the other inmates so he could get fresh batteries. The detective made up a variety of excuses and jail staff retrieved him at different times of the day to deflect attention away from their objective. The gamble paid off resulting in Laylah's murder being solved and those responsible for it being brought to justice. So, there we have it; detective Villarreal knew about a wire being used in a case he was involved in. Hence, I am faced with the same troubling question I had from the beginning: Why couldn't I wear a wire in my daughter's case? Better yet, who denied me that opportunity and for what reason?

After that setback, I reached out to the FBI. I obtained their field office number via public information. When I contacted 1-555-1212 and when I called a receptionist answered the phone. I told her my name and who I was. I asked her if I could speak with an agent and she said that I could only leave a message and someone would get back in touch with me. Feeling dejected for a moment I gave her my information and thanked her for what amounted to no help at all, then I ended the call. My solace was that I knew that I would eventually be getting some answers from the coldest and baddest organization on the planet. But to my surprise, I never got a response from them either.

Over the years I used to wonder why Elizabeth Smart got so much publicity and news coverage throughout the country and while Alexis received some attention, it wasn't nearly as much. I hate to play the race card but Alexis' case seems to have fostered a counterproductive approach by the police compared to other past Kidnappings of young children over the years.

Let me cite a couple of examples. Elizabeth Smart was taken out of her home, while Alexis was taken not even 100 yards from hers. Then there was the case of Polly Klaas who was also taken from her home and murdered (God rest her precious soul). The Governor of California at the time, Pete Wilson, spoke out adamantly about her case, while Wisconsin Governors who have been in office since Alexis disappeared, Jim Doyle, Scott Walker and now Tony Evers, have said nothing regarding Alexis. Granted Tony Evers just got into office, but believe that he too will remain silent about her case as well. It hurts me right down to my core and I just want answers from someone, somewhere, sometime.

This has been one long and stressful journey that has lasted for years now, with seemingly no direction to go in. Somebody or probably more than one somebody, knows the whereabouts of Alexis and what happened the morning she disappeared. Even more than that, I'll bet my life that it's the number one suspect who is the cause of my 22 Years of Hell: The Alexis Patterson Story! I will take all the suspicions I have about him to my grave. I am certain that he played a major role in Alexis' disappearance!

In summer of 2016, a young man named Josh, who was living in the state of Ohio, did something outlandish from a parent's perspective. Josh got angry at his ex-wife because she allegedly went out of town for a couple of days with another man. So, Josh took the children he and his ex-wife had together to the police station and made this claim: These are the children of Alexis Patterson, the little girl who went missing in Milwaukee, Wisconsin in 2002. For whatever reason, the police kept the children in their custody and when the young lady returned from her escapade, she learned where her children were and went to the police station to get them. She went by the name Lisa Miller.

The Ohio police got in contact with the Milwaukee police and sent pictures of Lisa to them. She looked very similar to the age enhanced photo the Milwaukee police had of Alexis. The media got a hold of this information and the story broke like wildfire and was spreading throughout social media and in breaking news stories in Wisconsin and Ohio. Everyone who saw Lisa Miller thought that it was Alexis; even my mother, adult children, siblings and some close friends. Lisa was also said to have some of the same body marking and scars that Alexis has. She was also known to have said that she does not have any recollection of her childhood before the age of ten. However, she did remember moving around a lot from state to state. This young lady was sounding more and more like she could actually be my Alexis! I was hopeful and excited at the prospect and I prayed to GOD that she was my precious Alexis!

Then came a bombshell, Lisa Miller said she was 28 years old when in actuality Alexis would only have been 21 years old in 2016 when all this took place. I thought, okay not a big deal since she said that she couldn't remember the first 10 years of her life. Then something else strange, her ex-husband's grandfather had to get her birth certificate for her when she and Josh got married. So, I was still very hopeful that Lisa was in fact Alexis.

Then the DNA test was conducted and despite all the similarities between Lisa and Alexis, the results showed that she was not Alexis. I was so broken and depressed but I have never given up on my mission to find Alexis, as my profound feelings that I've shared about her in this book demonstrate.

What I didn't understand is why the police used a 14-year-old toothbrush of Alexis' and not the blood from me and Alexis' mother to do the DNA test. It was also told to me that the two children also used Alexis' toothbrush when they spent the night over at her house on 49th St. In addition, every time Josh would make a Youtube video talking about the situation, his page would be shut down. He was also receiving death threats.

But Josh did get into contact with Alexis' mother via Facebook sometimes in the last week of June 2016. He even brought the kids he and Lisa had together all the way from Bryan, Ohio to Milwaukee. Alexis' mother took pictures with their children and everything and this was before the media broke the story about Lisa in July of 2016. Go figure.

I sent the police to Ohio in 2011 with information that Alexis was seen there in 2006, then Josh came out of nowhere with his claim about Lisa being Alexis and they lived in Ohio as well. All of these coincidences can't be without merit in my mind.

Josh's grandfather, who died of cancer, allegedly bought Lisa at a young age, had a child with her, then she and Josh got married when they became adults. Then they had a child of their own. After a while things started to fall apart with them and they divorced years later. Several years after that was when Josh got upset with Lisa and then the story of their lives together broke.

Again, I say that it all leads back to the number one suspect, who didn't talk to help bring Alexis home but he talked plenty to not go to prison with Booker.

And since Alexis' disappearance, I have been devastated by the events I've uncovered and the treachery I've learned that accompanied her life. I will never be the same because of this experience. I pray for strength and perseverance because at times I feel that I have exhausted all my remedies. Although I'm hurt and cut to the core, my determination and dedication to find Alexis remains steadfast and will do so until my casket drops.

CHAPTER 7
REFLECTIONS

Memories are one thing, dreams are another. Throughout the past decade and a half, the two have co-existed in my mind and in my soul and my life creating all kinds of emotions within me. Even though I'm not content with the situation surrounding my daughter, feelings of agony, heartache and discomfort find themselves faced with feelings of joy, happiness and optimism.

These feelings meet somewhere in the middle for me. That's my reality. The one thing about dreams is that you can wake up from them (GOD's willing) no matter how good or bad they are. Memories on the other hand are things that you participate in or witness that attach to you forever. They can also be good or bad. Believe me, over time you can forget dreams but memories are rarely forgotten. Especially when the images of those memories are the only things you have to hold on to. Things like a person, place or thing.

With that being said, it brings me to one time in 2003 when Fox News Channel 6 wanted to interview me. I will never forget this day because there was 3 or 4 inches of snow on the ground and it was Alexis' birthday. I had received a call from a news anchor/ reporter who worked at the net-work around noon. I was asked if I would be willing to talk with them on camera later that afternoon around 4 o'clock. I obliged and they wanted to conduct the interview at Alexis' school on the corner of 49th and Garfield where a little memorial had been set up in remembrance of my daughter.

I was visiting my sister Nicole, who was living on the other side of town on 103rd and Fond Du Lac, when I received that call from Fox News on my cell phone requesting to interview me. Truth be told, I don't know how the media obtained my cell number. When I asked about it, I was simply told, "We have our sources Mr. Campbell." I didn't push the issue; I was just thankful that Alexis would be getting some more exposure a year after her disappearance and that her story was being kept in headlines. As I was heading to Alexis' school from my sister's house around 3:30 in the afternoon, something ironic occurred to me. I was driving and listening to the radio when the DJ played a new ballad that Beyonce just released, Me, Myself and I and as I listened to the slow tempo cut, I realized that I was about to talk to the media by myself. I was alone and had to appeal to the world about how much I miss my baby. No one from my family or any of my friends were going to be present like they were in the beginning. It wasn't a major problem, I was just going to have to face society independently for the first time, expressing my feelings.

Midway to my destination I received a call from the anchor/reporter asking me if we could meet 30 minutes later than our scheduled time because they were running late. I told her it would be fine, then pulled to the side of the road and continued to listen to Beyonce sing that ballad. I was trying to decipher what she was singing about and the meaning behind the song. After the ballad was concluded, the station began playing some rap music. But I just wasn't in the mood for that, so I turned to another radio station and found that Beyonce's new hit was about to be played again. So, I pulled out into traffic and rode around a little bit, listening to this song that was apparently in heavy rotation throughout the airwaves. A few minutes before 4:30 pm I pulled up to Hi Mount Elementary School and parked on the corner of 49th and Garfield which was illegal.

The news network pulled up shortly after I did. Once they parked, we both exited our vehicles, greeted each other and I was thanked for meeting with them. I was told what I would be asked, then we walked toward the memorial. Upon approaching the memorial, I noticed that the site had a lot of trash laying around the reef and the stuffed animals that were placed there. So, my parental instinct kicked in and gathered all the mess that was scattered around and placed the paper, potato chip bags and other debris onto the floor of my sister's car in the back seat. What I didn't know at the time was that they filmed me cleaning my daughter's memorial area. Once I got back over to where the reef stood, the interview began. The anchor/reporter asked me how I felt and how I was doing and how I continued to deal with the situation surrounding Alexis' disappearance.

I told her that I was still hurting, but I was also very optimistic about finding my daughter. I explained that I was doing as well as could be expected under the circumstances and I expressed that I continuously deal with the situation by my faith in GOD, along with the support of my family, friends and the community.

However, my inspiration comes from my other children- Diamond, Madea, Kierre, Special, Promise, Kenya Jr. and Kenya III. Then the anchor/reporter asked me if Alexis was watching right now, what would you say to her? That's when I looked directly into the camera as if I were looking into her beautiful small dark brown eyes and said, "Alexis baby, daddy loves you with all my heart and soul and misses you so much- we all do. We're going to find you and bring you home!" Then the anchor/reporter said something to the effect of, "I'm such and such (her name) for Fox News, reporting." After the interview ended, I was thanked once more and told that this news segment would air that evening on the 6 o'clock news.

Now when you're dealing with people in the professional world, that be TV, radio, corporate America, etc., one has to pay attention to the words they use.

See, if I would have listened to what was said to me instead of just hearing what was said, I would have understood what was meant by the word segment. The word segment means: Any of the parts into which something can be divided. I didn't comprehend initially how the whole thing played out, with them being tardy and the wordplay she used until I saw the news story that night, so here is what I didn't know at that time. Check it out.

When I was told that they were running late, it was because they were filming Alexis' birthday party that her mother was having for her at the Washington Park Pavilion. It was a celebration of her 8th birthday. I also didn't know that they filmed me cleaning off the memorial site because the interview hadn't started until I came back across the street from putting the garbage in the car so I could discard it later. So, when I saw the split Tv screen of me picking up litter at my daughter's memorial and the celebration Alexis' mother was having for her, I was like whoa. I didn't take offense, I just looked at it as they were showing two different parents, doing two different things, on the birthday of their missing child. I was mourning and cleaning the area where she might have been last, while the other parent was celebrating. I, myself, never attended those parties because they would have been too emotional for me. The vigils were hard enough and sad enough for me to get through. I just couldn't bring myself to celebrate at a party without Alexis being there.

Now allow me to share this memory of Alexis that I cherish along with so many others. This was in the summer of 2001 and I was dropping Alexis off over to her great grandmother, Ms. Betty, who owned a house on

6th and Burleigh. As usual Alexis had spent the weekend over by my house, but that Sunday we went to my mother's before it had gotten too dark to visit. So as the day turned to night, I was dropping Alexis off first because Ms. Betty's house was less than a mile from my mother's in route to taking my other kids Madea, Kierre and Special home. Promise and Kenya Jr. were babies and already at home with my girl.

When we pulled up in front of Ms. Betty's house, Alexis asked if she could stay and watch TV while I took her siblings home. I had a burgundy 1994 Fleetwood Cadillac with a booming ass sound system and 3 TV's I had just put in. Anyone could hear my music slamming for blocks away. My mother would tell me all the time when I arrived on her block to turn my music off or way down, because she didn't want to hear "all that noise" as she put it. Anyway, I told Alexis not this time but next time I would drop everyone else off first, then she could stay and watch TV. For now, though, she was the first rugrat off the ship. Her reply to that was, "Shute." Everyone said their goodbyes to Alexis and hugged her before she exited the car. Then I walked her up the steps to the porch and knocked on the door. A little girl who was about Alexis' age appeared in the big glass picture window that was part of the door and became excited because she saw Alexis. She began jumping up and down and smiling, saying, "Alexis, Alexis!" It was just another example of the effect she had on people. The little girl opened the door and assumed it was her cousin because that's all that was over by Ms. Betty's house. That includes every home Ms. Betty had ever lived in.

Through all the years and all the residences Ms. Betty lived in, all who were over by her were family members as far as I can recall. From the house she had on Hopkins and Villard where Alexis' mother lived when we met, to the house on 42nd and Concordia where Alexis was conceived and onto the house on 17th and Capitol where Alexis was born, it was about being surrounded by family to Ms. Betty. And now the same was true at the house on 6th and Burleigh.

The little girl opened the door and when Alexis walked in, she hugged Alexis. After the 2 of them hugged, Alexis turned to give me a kiss. I kissed her, then told her I loved her. The little girl had to be really eager because before Alexis could finish getting out her "I love you" to me, her cousin was pulling Alexis out of the threshold and closing the door on me. I heard Alexis saying, "Girl, don't close the door on my daddy." Then Alexis hurried and opened the door back up. It kind of blew me away seeing how protective she was of me. I told Alexis that it was okay and that her cousin was just happy to see her. Then I reached in my pocket and gave Alexis and her cousin five dollars apiece.

One time I had a sweet tooth, so I pulled into the parking lot of Fast and Friendly. It's a store that sits on the corner of Locust and Martin Luther King Dr. Once inside the store I picked up some barbeque chips, slow poke suckers, hot tamales, grape now & laters, some blunts for my adult pleasure and orange juice. I gave the young lady at the checkout one of several Andrew Jackson's I had to pay for the items, when I suddenly got a call on my cell that one of my homeboys was fighting some chump in front of my house who was from up the block. I already had one of the suckers in my mouth, so I grabbed the bag off the counter and told the young lady to keep the change. Then I dashed toward the door. Running to my ride, I saw the number one suspect and Alexis' mother pull up next to my Cadillac.

When I made it to the driver's door of my ride, I noticed Alexis was in the back seat of their car next to the number one suspect's son. I spoke to them because it was a cordial thing to do. Then stuck my head through the back seat window and leaned toward Alexis. "Hey baby, give yo' daddy a kiss," I said to her. Alexis kissed me and asked if she could have some candy. I had to take the sucker out of my mouth to kiss her so she knew I was holding. Since I was in a hurry, I took the blunts out of the bag and then put the whole bag in her lap. "Wow!" she said. She had a big ol'

Chester Cheetah smile on her face that I'll never forget. I told her to share it with "little man" which is what I called the number one suspect's son because I didn't know his name. Then I told her I loved her and would see her later. Alexis said, "I love you too daddy." I addressed the couple again and then I slid into the soft cushion seats of my Cadillac to head to the drama that lay ahead.

That fight sprawled into the next day in which my downstairs neighbor Sean ended up getting popped in the shoulder. His cousin Twan ended up getting murderers several months later because of that atrocious altercation. Sean died a few years later from an asthma attack. May they both rest in peace.

I truly believe that Alexis could have been anything she wanted in life. I say that because of the effect she had on everyone who had the privilege of meeting her or spending any amount of quality time with her. Any such person would have wanted to help, assist or just be a part of anything she had going on in life as she progressed from childhood to adulthood. I also believed she could have been an entertainer like a comedian for example because she was naturally funny with the things she used to say.

Which brings me to a day that it was hot outside and we were having a blast with the water hose over at my mother's house. Before I got to spraying everybody with water, Alexis came up to me and said, "Daddy, don't get my hair wet because my mama just did it and it's looking very nice. So, I said, "Alexis, what, you don't think my mama and sisters know how to do hair? And since you are trying to cop a plea, here take this." I sprayed her from head to toe. When she screamed, I didn't know if it was because the water was too cold or if it was because of her pretty hairdo getting wet. After the water combat, which included anything that could contain water or that could throw water, I had my sister Angie, who was 12 at the time, redo Alexis' hair. Once Angie had finished with Alexis' hair and I saw it, I walked up on Alexis and told her that I should have taken her advice and not wet her hair. Then she gave me a look as if to say, "I told you so." It was priceless.

I had soooo many memories that I cherish with Alexis in such a short time but I'm so very blessed to know her, to love her and I want the world to know about her through the pages of this book. She was: Always, Lively, Enthusiastic, Xylitol, Innocent, Sweetness. That's what ALEXIS means to me and what she was still is. That's how I remember her. Now these are my reflections…

March 6, 2017 was a very exciting day in my life for 2 reasons. First, Kenya III turned 15 years old and we had a meaningful father to son conversation. He had some issues that he was dealing with and I gave him my expertise in order to come up with some solutions to remedy them. I was blessed that GOD gave me the intellect to reach Kenya III with the wisdom of encouragement, inspiration and especially love.

Also on that day, GOD bestowed another blessing upon me that was a long time in coming. The nationally syndicated TV show Crime Watch Daily, that comes on Monday-Friday on NBC at 2 o'clock, aired a little recap of Alexis's story. I was very happy, excited and pretty emotional as well because it had been a long time since Alexis received national exposure. One of the last times her case garnered national attention was when America's Most Wanted previewed her case but that show had been off the air for like 10 years now. Nevertheless, I was thankful that my daughter's disappearance was brought back into the living rooms of America once again. The coverage allowed her case to be fresh on people's minds after a decade and a half. My prayer is that this time around the results from this showing will generate a prestigious outcome for me and those who miss Alexis dearly.

In closing I would just like to say: PARENTS, know who you have around your children, please! And even more than that, be vigilant and stay involved with every aspect of their lives. Yours kids might get a little upset with you because of all the extra attention as they get older but there's no substitute for peace of mind! It doesn't matter where you live or the kind of neighborhood you reside in, this kind of thing can happen anywhere, anytime, to anyone. I say all this because I truly care about every parent and child across this country and I don't want anyone to have to endure what I have had to go through for all these years now. Take care and GOD bless.

Now, for those who are in the streets: It's only a game when you're playing it, but remember that it's real life when the drama hits. So whatever hand you're dealt, respect it and accept it.

I'm ending with a few lyrics from the song I wrote after Alexis' disappearance. For those of you who find themselves in the same unfortunate circumstances as myself, I'm sure you can feel my pain just as I feel yours as well. GOD bless you all. May GOD keep you and make his face shine upon you and give you peace. This song is for you Alexis:

Alexis

She's the 4th of daddy's 9 and always on my mind, although I'm stressed, I'm blessed, faced dealing with some hard times, Everybody in the city knows about my business, so I'm keep it real with y'all and tell you how I'm feeling, Incomplete, lost only God knows, I thank Him every day for keeping my actions in Control, touching my soul, cock back ready for war, won't discriminate, eliminate who played a role, I never did like the police, but I'ma bow down and be a pal, working with them until I get my child found, only in the first grade, hoping that she ran away, cause she couldn't take to school some treats on her snack day, You gave her one anyway, but you don't know I knew that though and I wonder why you didn't stress that on them talk shows, what you got to hide? Bet it's eating you alive staying silent when you should be talking, that ain't wise (Chorus)

Lord, keep my baby safe, Tell her it's gonna be okay, soon she'll be back around to smile in her daddy's face Shelter her, comfort her, keep your' arms around her I'll leave it up in yo' hands Heavenly Father
(chorus) x2

EPILOGUE

I always wondered how Scott Peterson was arrested and held for the murder of his wife Laci and their unborn child Connor without proof of his guilt or involvement. It puzzled me so much that I actually called Modesto, California and got a hold of the sheriff's department where Scott was being held without bail in 2003. I found out that he had been caught traveling with $15,000 and was only 30 miles from the Mexican border while his picture and that of his beautiful wife Laci, played on television all across America during the time of her disappearance. What I was having trouble comprehending was how Scott could be arrested and held in jail when at the time it was only speculated that Laci was missing.

The number one suspect was the last person to be with my daughter before she was categorized as missing also. So why wasn't he arrested and put in jail like Scott was?

So, me, not being one to sit still where my daughter is concerned, called out west to see if the police there could explain to me why Scott was being detained and the number one suspect was free to roam the streets. I was put on hold for about 20 minutes but I swear it felt like forever. The elevator music playing while I waited but did little to calm my nerves and emotions. When a deputy finally did come on line, I got straight to the point and asked why Scott was detained. I was told that they couldn't disclose that information. So, I said, "Look, I'm calling from Milwaukee, Wisconsin and my daughter was last seen with her mother's husband and has been missing for a year. Please explain to me why isn't the guy in jail like Scott Peterson?! The deputy told me that he was sorry about the situation involving my daughter Alexis but different states have jurisdictions and handle cases differently. What I didn't know at the time was that investigators had all kinds of evidence on Scott in addition to what I already knew. Evidence that had not been disclosed to the public that was sufficient to lock him up. Some of that evidence was his alibi not matching up with what he told detectives and the revelation that he had a mistress, Amber Frey, who told police about all the lies Scott told her regarding Laci. However, not getting the answers I would have liked, I ended the phone call.

What the deputy told me about different states having different jurisdictions and handling cases differently, kept going through my mind as I sat on my couch. Just like Scott was a suspect in Laci's disappearance, I also was a suspect in Alexis' disappearance. We were both followed by law enforcement for a while, as the number one suspect. As I look back on that now, I don't see anything different between Scott's situation and my own but I do see the difference as far as the evidence is concerned. The authorities had nothing on me, but in Scott's case, they had a lot of circumstantial evidence linking him to Laci's disappearance.

Now let me expose the number one suspect's situation:

He was the last person to see Alexis, his story of what took place the morning she disappeared kept changing, he failed a polygraph test and he continued to beat Alexis' mother. That's quite a bit of circumstantial evidence to continue to allow the number one suspect to roam free. Then there is the word "different" which doesn't apply here. Scott lied; the number one suspect lied.

Scott changed his story too. There is no difference between these two men except that one is on death row in California and the other is on the streets of Milwaukee. Scott was trying to flee to another country while under surveillance and despite having only circumstantial case against him, the Modesto Police Department wasn't just going to allow him to cross the border. I wish the Milwaukee Police Department had that same attitude. I sure would like to give a dose of reality to whoever said, "Time heals all wounds."

I'd like to have that person walk in the shoes I've been walking in for the past 17-plus years now.

During the 5th year after Alexis disappeared, I did an interview for the Milwaukee Journal Sentinel with a reporter by the name of Jesse Garza. In that interview Mr. Garza asked me how I was doing 5 years to the day Alexis disappeared, which was coming up in a couple of days. In my anguish I gave him this answer from my heart, "After all these years, the pain doesn't get better, it just gets worse."

Alexis' disappearance is the biggest missing persons case in the history of the Milwaukee Police Department to date. Not knowing is the salt that's poured on my broken heart every single day. I appreciate Jesse Garza because that interview continued to give Alexis' case exposure over the years she's been missing.

What I thought was inappropriate however, was when I read the article the next day and saw that Mr. Garza had added the situation the number one suspect was involved in concerning his participation in that 1994 bank robbery I wrote about earlier in the book. It read, "Mr. Bourgeois, who received immunity for his involvement in a 1994 bank robbery that resulted in the fatal shooting of Glendale police officer Ronald Hedbany," so on and so forth. I don't know if Mr. Garza was doing an ass-assination of the number one suspect's character or not but what I do know is that I thought it was tasteless and insensitive. I'll even go so far as to say that it was disrespectful to mention in an article that was meant to be for the expressing of my feelings, thoughts and optimism about Alexis' case. I guess any exposure is better than no exposure when you're fighting for a cause of information that's relevant to you. That cause being my precious jewel, Alexis. As you can imagine, I have had so many highs and lows in the early years of my daughter's absence and the years that followed later. As I wrote in the book, Alexis' disappearance made national headlines across the country.

I was on several talk radio stations such as 860 WNOV, 620 WTMJ and 1130 (I don't remember their call sign). I also appeared on every local TV news outlet and gave separate interviews to each network throughout all these years talking about Alexis, just as I did when I appeared on talk radio. I was even on a syndicated cable TV news show.

Out of all the broadcasting entities and organizations that featured or covered my daughter's story, it never occurred to me who was being compassionate and who just wanted ratings. I assumed they were being sympathetic and genuine, until I noticed 2 situations where it seemed like it was more about publicity than anything else. I felt both situations were truly surreal.

I remember that during the first month of Alexis' disappearance, members of the Nation of Islam appeared on the news stating that they were now the official spokesman for Alexis' family, while Alexis' mother and the number one suspect stood right beside them at the podium. A few weeks later, I never heard from the Nation of Islam again. To this day I often wonder why that was? Then there was time in the summer of 2002 or 2003 that this telepathist, who had a national TV show, whose name was John Claud, showed up. I forgot his last name but he had red hair with a red bushy mustache. Anyway, he got in touch with Alexis' mother and told her that he had a premonition about Alexis and wanted to come to Milwaukee and show us where her body could be found.

Needless to say, on the day he was to come to Milwaukee, he called and said something more important came up and that he had to cancel the appearance. The nerve of that jerk! Like what could be more important than helping my daughter's mother and I find our baby? Then to add insult to injury, he never called back to reschedule. But I do recall a few situations that touched my heart and let me know that my family and I weren't alone in this horrific ordeal.

One gentleman by the name of Keith Martin started the LAP (Locate Alexis Patterson) organization. They handed out fliers and did searches throughout the city. Hundreds of people who weren't even part of LAP helped with fliers and searches as well and I want to acknowledge them also. Some time later LAP changed its name from Locate Alexis Patterson to Location Assistance Professionals. That was a nice gesture on their part.

Mr. John Robbins-Well was a retired private investigator who volunteered his services too. He spent many, many hours sitting in front of a computer, updating the operation-lap.org website. He listened to police scanners and talked with people even though he was 65 years of age. Then came some support and acts of kindness out of the city of Madison, our state capitol.

In 2005, the city of Madison was hosting a ceremony for missing people throughout the entire state. Families of the missing were invited to attend and received a candle and a memorial certificate. Alexis' mother was invited but unfortunately, she couldn't attend. That left the chair that had Alexis' picture on it empty. This soulful lady that we (Alexis' Family) didn't know, felt that she should become a member of Alexis' family that day. So, she occupied the chair and accepted the candle and certificate on behalf of the Alexis Patterson family. May GOD bless her soul. I found out about this ceremony a couple of weeks after it happened. I wanted to express my appreciation and gratitude and I also wanted a candle and a copy of the memorial certificate. So, I wrote to the individual who orchestrated the gathering- which happened to be Wisconsin State Attorney General Peggy A. Lautenschlager.

A week after I reached out to her in a letter I received a copy of the ceremony program, which listed all the missing persons pictures and information on it. Also included was a duplicate certificate about Alexis. I never had any interactions with Arthur Jones, who was Milwaukee's police chief at the time Alexis disappeared or David Clarke who was the sheriff. But the highest law enforcement official in the state of Wisconsin acknowledged who I was, responded to my heartfelt request and provided me with more than I asked for in that response. Ms. Lautenschlager did all this even though I was incarcerated at the time. That not only meant a lot to me personally but it showed Ms. Lautenschlager's humanity and character. I have the utmost respect for her and I will never forget her generosity toward me.

As long as I have air in my lungs and a heartbeat, I will continue with my search for Alexis. I can't express with mere words how much desire, passion, intensity, drive and willingness I have within me to find my precious daughter. So much so that in October 2017, when I spoke with detectives, they asked me if I heard anything new concerning Alexis. (Throughout the investigation I always gave them things to look into). I told them no and that if I did find out something new that I would share it with them. Then I reminded them that if I had been allowed to wear a wire for a meeting with the number one suspect a few years earlier - a meeting that he requested - maybe something new would have been discovered.

I knew that I had to be of some relevance to them because they kept asking if I had any new information on a semi-regular basis. Truth be told is that because of my overwhelming desire to find Alexis, I have made myself relevant! And I will always be relevant when it comes to the search for Alexis! In the words made famous by entrepreneur/mogul Sean P. Diddy Combs,

"I CAN'T STOP, WON'T STOP!"

AUTHOR'S NOTE

I wrote this book in the hope that it will serve a couple of purposes: First, that it will encourage someone to come forward with new information about Alexis' disappearance. Second, to help ensure that what happened to Alexis never happens to another child anywhere, at any time. And finally, it is my hope that the information I divulged in this book will bring renewed awareness to the plight of missing children and their families everywhere.

By staying involved with what is going on with both the police and talking to people on their own, I believe families in this situation will increase the chances of their missing loved ones coming home to them. I hope my story about my missing daughter will be an example of how to do that. If my efforts and the efforts of others saves even one child who has disappeared, then my daughter's situation will not be in vain. If there is anything I would like to leave you, the readers and the wonderful people who helped and supported me and my family by allowing Alexis into your hearts, homes and thoughts, it would be a profound and heartfelt thank you. Your care, concern and prayers mean more to me than mere words can say. God bless all of you and please continue to keep my daughter in your prayers and in your hearts.

- AMEN -

ACKNOWLEDGEMENTS

I would like to pay homage and convey my sincere appreciation as I extend a special THANK YOU to the following individuals:

My mother, Ms. Cynthia Campbell, for her support and unconditional love. I love you with all my heart and soul. My siblings, Gary (Jr.), Nicole (Nikki Mac), Angela (B Angie B) and Alisha. Although I'm the big bro, all of you have been there for me. My grandma, Lorraine Ruffin (Mitt), who embraced me with love and open arms. I have not forgotten the time when I was on the run back in 1992 for that city bus incident and your house was surrounded by the Milwaukee County Sheriff's Department. Mitt, I always wondered why you didn't get mad at me. My godmother Deborah, I love you ma. My other siblings, Natasha (Tasha), Tequilla (Quilla), De'osha (Dee Dee), Stephon and Lorainz (Pubba).

My cousin Marqueda, you came through for your cousin Alexis on 49th St., washing dishes, preparing food and cleaning for her mother as she mourned.

Much love. Eric Roach (Eee), Kevin Cooper (Coupe), King Macho and Jason Wilks (J-Bone). You came through like you said you would and reached for me. Love homie and I haven't forgotten about that nah'mean.

Milwaukee's own R&B singer Rodney Poe. My homeboy Gleen Dixon, Ms. Jamie Underwood, Matisha Davis (TiTo), you never gave me ANY drama involving our handsome son. You've been A-1 since Day-1. Thank you.

My seeds from the oldest to the youngest: Diamond, Madea, Kierre, Alexis, Special, aPromise, Kenya Jr., Kenya III, Treasure, Tany'e Serenity, and R.I.P. Jody. Also, a special thank you to Dennis Warren Jr. (Bless), you know what you did. I'm indebted to you bro. And Mr. Anthony Horton a.k.a (Ace Boogie); what you did for Alexis and myself was very much appreciated. Love, big homie.

Thank you to my true friend, who I am honored to have known and who has been my greatest confidant, Dr. Gena Clark-McKnight. Thank you for listening and building me up when I was at a low point in my life. I love you for the person you are, who is strong and humble, despite what you have gone through.

Now a thank you to those who have passed on from this life: My cousin Denett Dyson R.I.P. I miss you so much. Alonza Patterson (Azonla) R.I.P., Hot Boy Lil' Cee R.I.P. granddad Big Robert R.I.P. uncle Buck R.I.P. grandma Mary Perkins and granddad William Perkins R.I.P.
And last but most definitely not least, thank you to my LORD AND SAVIOR FATHER GOD! All I have I was blessed with by YOU!

THE STORY

In 2016, news networks both locally and nationally, and social media reported a sighting of my beautiful angel in the state of Ohio.

Three seasons (8 months) after the nation mourned the 9 -11 attacks, another tragedy struck in the midwestern area of the country. The location was Milwaukee Wisconsin, and the victim was a little 7-year-old girl named Alexis S. Patterson, my daughter. It's sad when something like this happens anywhere, but when Alexis went missing, it triggered a city-wide manhunt.

The suspect pool was anyone living in the city of Milwaukee. Law enforcement presumptuously stated that, "Anyone blood related, or that is close to the person, is a chief suspect." However, the leading suspect was a man deeply entangled in the dark elements of the criminal underworld. It is a man who has been overlooked for years, but I knew better than to do that.

IN THE PRESS

Friday October 16, 1992   ⋆

Madison High School

Officers search for youth who fired shots from bus

By KEVIN HARRINGTON
and ANNE BOTHWELL
of The Journal staff

Milwaukee County sheriff's officers went to Madison High School Friday morning looking for the teen who fired shots from a county bus Thursday.

No one was in custody Friday morning.

The 28-year-old man who was driving the bus at the time of the shooting accompanied sheriff's deputies on their trip to the school Friday, in hopes he could help identify a suspect, said a spokeswoman from the Milwaukee County Transit System.

Several gunshots were fired from the bus Thursday in an incident authorities believe was gang-related.

The bus driver told authorities that he was taking on passengers at W. Fond du Lac Ave. and W. Capitol Drive about 2:55 p.m. when occupants of a car alongside the bus flashed gang signals to at least one of about 37 students on the bus.

A teenage male on the bus returned gang hand signals, and a passenger in the car waved a handgun, authorities said. A youth on the bus then fired as many as six shots at the car. No injuries were reported.

The bus driver pulled away from the intersection and drove southeast on W. Fond du Lac Ave. The teenage male flipped open an emergency window and jumped out of the bus. The bus stopped at W. Fond du Lac Ave. and N. Sherman Blvd.

"We were just getting on the bus," said a 16-year-old girl from Marshall High School, who asked that her name not be used. "Everyone was hyped, scared. They we're yelling 'They're shooting. They're shooting.'"

Milwaukee police, sheriff's deputies and members of the Milwaukee Public Schools security team responded. Students from Madison and Marshall High Schools were on the bus at the time, authorities said.

School district spokeswoman Karen Salzbrenner said: "If the suspect is one of our students, my concern would be that he might have had that gun in school with him all day. This is a good example of the urgency with which we need to begin implementing weapons searches."

The School Board last month approved plans to allow principals to conduct random weapons searches of middle and high school students.

Journal reporter Phil Nero contributed to this story.

I met Alexis's mother four months after this incident while serving county time with Huber privileges. A year later Alexis was born.

Dahmer killings

Victims' families want officers to stay fired

They say rehiring 2 in botched encounter would be an injustice

By KATHERINE M. SKIBA
of The Journal staff

Relatives of Jeffrey Dahmer's murder victims want the two Milwaukee police officers who botched an early encounter with the serial killer to stay fired.

"They want the officers fired, and they want to get the public involved in making sure the Fire and Police Commission knows that," said Art Murchison, a spokesman for the family members.

The officers are Joseph Gabrish, 29, and John Balcerzak, 35. They pleaded guilty this week to failure to conduct a proper investigation during an encounter with 14-year-old victim Konerak Sinthasomphone and Dahmer in May 1991.

The two officers returned the dazed and injured boy, who had escaped from the serial killer, to Dahmer's care. The murders of Konerak and the other victims were not discovered until July 1991.

Balcerzak and Gabrish were fired, but they have appealed that action. Their dismissals will be reviewed at a meeting of the Fire and Police Commission Oct. 27.

Murchison runs a support group for the families at Career Youth Development, a social service agency at 2601 N. King Drive.

He said four relatives gathered Thursday in a special meeting of the support group, and he has had contact with three others by phone. They are related to these victims: Tony Hughes, Oliver Lacy, Ernest Miller, Richard Guerrero and Eddie Smith.

"They didn't believe there would be any successes without justice, and they didn't believe there would be justice unless these officers are fired," Murchison said.

Public demonstrations and news conferences are being considered, Murchison said.

POLICE-MINORITY RELATIONS

According to Murchison, the believe that advances in police-minority relations would be set back if the officers are rehired.

The botched encounter and the murders cut like a knife through minority communities. Old wounds are recalled, too.

This, for a few reasons: the teen was Laotian; the people who tried to get help for him were African-American; and most of Dahmer's murder victims were African-American, American Indian or Hispanic.

As a result, Murchison said, the relatives don't view the case of the two officers in isolation. One relative — he said he doesn't remember who — said that to give the officers a lesser penalty would be "a return to Breierism."

That refers to former Police Chief Harold A. Breier, who some regarded as racist. He retired in 1984 after a long career.

Another relative, Murchison said, has resurrected the memory of Ernest Lacy, a black man who died in Milwaukee police custody in 1981. Lacy wrongly had been arrested for rape.

"We have to call a spade a spade in Milwaukee: It's not like Selma, Ala., in the '60s, but we have institutional racism," Murchison said.

He added, though, that minorities were impressed with Police Chief Philip Arreola and his bid for sensitivity training and introducing new recruits to the central city.

"The strides he is attempting to make in our community cannot be successful if the community doesn't feel a sense of trust," Murchison said.

Dahmer killed 17 men and boys and now is serving multiple life prison terms.

Greenfield library offers program on Faberge

Greenfield — Adults are invited to a program on Faberge egg art at 10 a.m. Oct. 24 at the Greenfield Public Library, 7215 W. Cold Spring Road.

Donna Marie Runge, artist and lecturer, will talk about Carl Faberge. The program is free. Those interested should call the library at 321-0505.

This whole situation was a horrible thing.
I pray for the victims and their family.

Alexis Patterson might now look something like this image from the National Center for Missing and Exploited Children.

This image of Alexis was plastered on fliers.

Kenya Campbell, Alexis Patterson's father, has hope his daughter is alive. "But still, I wonder what she looks like, if she's being taken care of...." With him is his sister, Nicole Campbell, in front of her north side home.

JESSE GARZA /
JGARZA@JOURNAL-
SENTINEL.COM

5 years ago, Alexis Patterson disappeared. Her father has anguished over his daughter since, but he holds hope she's still alive.

Pain 'just gets worse'

By JESSE GARZA
jgarza@journalsentinel.com

The first time he ever heard his daughter Alexis Patterson's name on television in May 2002, Kenya Campbell was an inmate in the Milwaukee County House of Correction.

He saw TV cameras focused on her mother, Ayanna Patterson, and stepfather, LaRon Bourgeois, several days after Alexis was reported missing as they pleaded for the return of the 7-year-old Milwaukee girl.

In the following days and months, he would hear and see her name countless times on television and in print. He'd see her disappearance lead to a massive search involving hundreds of volunteers and become one of the biggest missing person cases in the history of the Milwaukee Police Department.

He'd see the image of the smiling first-grader with the braided, beaded hair on "missing" fliers throughout the city.

And in the years leading to Thursday's fifth anniversary of her unsolved disappearance, he would watch in anguish as that image became seared into the city's psyche.

"After all these years, the pain doesn't get better, it just gets worse," Campbell said in an interview this week.

Campbell, 33, a construction worker, hasn't given up hope that his daughter is still alive.

"But still, I wonder what she looks like, if she's being taken care of... or if she's being abused."

Alexis' stepfather, Bourgeois, told police he last saw the girl crossing the street after walking her a half-block from their home to Hi-Mount Elementary School, 4921 W. Garfield Ave.

Police extensively questioned Bourgeois and Ayanna Patterson but never connected either of them to Alexis' disappearance.

In subsequent interviews with the press, Bourgeois, who received immunity for his involvement in a 1994 bank robbery that resulted in the fatal shooting of Glendale Police Officer Ronald Hedbany, angrily de-

Please see ALEXIS, 6B

153

From page 1

ALEXIS

Hope kept alive

nied any role in the girl's disappearance.

Attempts to locate the couple, whose divorce was finalized in February 2005, were unsuccessful.

Large-scale investigation

More Milwaukee police resources were allocated for the investigation into Alexis' disappearance than the Jeffrey Dahmer case, said Deputy Chief Brian O'Keefe, who, as a captain with the Criminal Investigation Bureau, was involved in Alexis' case.

O'Keefe said the investigation was second in size only to the case of Quadrevion Henning, 12, and Purvis Virginia Parker, 11, two Milwaukee boys whose bodies were found in the McGovern Park lagoon in April 2006 after being missing for almost a month.

"In both of those investigations, on some days we literally had more than 100 officers and detectives working," said O'Keefe, who noted that foul play was not involved in the boys' deaths.

During the initial search for Alexis, officers worked on their days off and O'Keefe's department received assistance from the FBI and other local and state law enforcement agencies, he said.

"When it comes to kids, everyone wants to do what they can and hopes that it's going to turn out all right," he said. "Regrettably, that wasn't the case in this instance."

Reward still offered

Milwaukee County Sheriff David A. Clarke Jr. assigned 15 detectives to the investigation, and his department used drug forfeiture money to put up a $10,000 reward for information leading to Alexis, a reward that is still being offered today.

"I'm surprised that, in the aftermath, nothing has come out by now," said Clarke, who believes foul play is involved in the disappearance.

"I believe it's criminal in nature and in the criminal world information will come out," he said.

"Somebody knows something about this child."

The case has been featured on television shows from "America's Most Wanted" to CNN and Fox News.

Last October Ayanna Patterson described her pain during an interview on the Maury Povich show.

"The last four years of my life have been a nightmare," she said. "I'm so empty."

According to sources familiar with the case, a John Doe investigation into Alexis' disappearance was launched in January 2003, though that has never been officially confirmed.

Campbell said his images of "Lexis" will always include those of her carrying her baby brother around on her hip, eating pizzas and staying up late watching movies during visits.

"I wouldn't wish this kind of hurt on anyone," he said, adding that, no matter what led to Alexis' disappearance, he wants anyone who knows anything about it to remember two things.

"She is completely innocent," he said. "And she's just a child."

■

I felt that the #1 suspects bank robbery involvement resulting in the death of a police officer was inappropriate for this particular new article.

154

"Elizabeth is happy, she is well, and we are so happy to have her back in our arms."

Ed Smart, father of kidnapped girl

Smart had to depend on captors, police say

When found, Salt Lake teen denied her identity

By PATTY HENETZ
Associated Press

Salt Lake City — Trapped in the hills above her anguished family's home for the first two months of her disappearance, Elizabeth Smart may have been kept from escaping or crying out for help by the growing influence of her captors, police said Thursday.

Frightened at first by her abduction at knifepoint, Elizabeth was forced to depend on her captors during her nine-month disappearance, authorities said. When found by police, the 15-year-old vehemently denied her identity when asked whether she was Elizabeth Smart, and told officers that the couple she was with were her parents.

"There is clearly a psychological impact that occurred at some point," Police Chief Rick Dinse said. "There is no question that she was psychologically affected."

Salt Lake police briefly outlined Elizabeth's movements over the nine months, saying she spent the first two months held by Brian Mitchell and Wanda Barzee, achingly close to home in Dry Creek Canyon, a popular hiking area searched many times in the summer.

In October, the three rode a bus to San Diego, and the group returned to the Salt Lake area Wednesday, the day of their capture in the suburb of Sandy, police said.

Hours after she vanished, while in Dry Creek Canyon, Elizabeth had heard one of her uncles calling out her name but was unable to respond, her family said.

Back in their arms

Thursday, her family and friends focused not on what

could have been but on the astounding event many were calling a miracle: Elizabeth, taken from her bed in the middle of the night, was home again, playing the harp and watching her favorite movie, "The Trouble with Angels."

"Elizabeth is happy, she is well, and we are so happy to have her back in our arms," said her beaming father, Ed Smart.

Sierra Smart said she and several other cousins in the devout and affluent Mormon family spent about three hours with Elizabeth during her first full day at home. "She's, like, totally talking, totally casual," said Sierra, 22. "She got all new clothes. She gave a fashion show."

Ed Smart said he 'had not

pressed his daughter for details of her captivity. "What is going to come out is going to come out," he said. "I don't have it in me to try and make this harder for her than it is."

Asked how she had changed, he said she had returned home "really a young woman."

Dressed in a wig, veil and sunglasses, Elizabeth told the police officers who picked her up with Mitchell and his wife, Barzee, that her name was "Augustine."

Police questioned her aggressively about her identity, Officer Bill O'Neal said. He said she became agitated when officers asked her to remove her wig and sunglasses and told them she recently had eye surgery.

"We took her aside ... she

kind of just blurted out, 'I know who you think I am. You guys think I'm that Elizabeth Smart girl who ran away,'" O'Neal said.

"Her heart was beating so hard you could see it through her chest," he said.

Mitchell, a 49-year-old panhandler and self-proclaimed prophet for the homeless who fancied himself a polygamist, and Barzee remained jailed Thursday on suspicion of aggravated kidnapping.

Authorities in California disclosed Thursday that he had been arrested and held for six days in San Diego County last month for vandalizing a church.

Deputies had no reason to keep him in custody in that

case, sheriff's spokesman Chris Saunders said. Mitchell pleaded guilty and was released on probation Feb. 18.

"If we had to do it over again, there's really nothing different we could have done, because Salt Lake City authorities didn't identify him as a suspect until March 1," Saunders said.

Hiding in plain sight

For much of the time she was gone, it now appears Elizabeth was hiding in plain sight, sometimes swathed in robes and veils.

She also may have spent time in an apartment a block from a Salt Lake City police station, and attended a party in the company of her apparent abductors.

Daniel Trotta, who says he unknowingly sheltered Elizabeth and the drifter couple in a Salt Lake City apartment for several days in the fall, claims the girl never expressed fear and had opportunities to escape or at least call police.

Police have refused to confirm Trotta's account. A Smart family spokesman said Elizabeth never had a chance to slip away because she was always with Mitchell and Barzee.

Police said Thursday that they made mistakes in their nine-month effort to find Elizabeth, fixing on the wrong suspects and withholding a composite sketch of the man now being held in her abduction.

They focused much of their investigation on handyman Richard Ricci, 48, hired by the Smarts to help remodel their home. He was in jail for a parole violation when he died in August after suffering a brain hemorrhage.

Dinse acknowledged investigators were slow to release a sketch of Mitchell, whom Elizabeth's sister had suggested was the abductor.

"Hindsight is 20-20 vision. If we had to go back over it again, I think every one of (our investigators) would say, 'I wish we had gone public with that ... earlier,'" Dinse said.

Elizabeth Smart stands with her parents, Lois and Ed, outside their Utah home Thursday. Elizabeth, 15, who disappeared from her home in June, was found by police Wednesday.

ASSOCIATED PRESS

Elizabeth Smart had a lot of national exposure and I'm pleased that her family had a happy ending. Alexis received lots of local exposure but not much national coverage. Elizabeth was abducted from Utah and as you see here she made the Milwaukee newspaper.

Stepdad accused of hitting wife

He also threatened to kill mother of missing child, complaint alleges

By DAVID DOEGE
ddoege@journalsentinel.com

The stepfather of Alexis Patterson, a Milwaukee girl missing for nearly a year, was charged Tuesday with beating the girl's mother and threatening to kill her.

Laron C. Bourgeois was charged in a criminal complaint that says his wife, Ayanna Patterson, told police he has become abusive and controlling and "has not comforted her during the very difficult time of the disappearance of her daughter."

Bourgeois even became angry, at one point last week when Alexis' mother told him that a detective was coming to their home with some information regarding the missing girl, complaining, "What the (expletive) does he want? I don't give a (expletive) about (him)," according to the complaint.

Bourgeois' wife also accused her husband of "using and selling drugs" and "pimping several other women," according to the complaint.

Bourgeois, 35, of the 1300 block of N. 43rd St., was charged in the complaint with battery and disorderly conduct while armed.

Alexis was last seen about 7:40 a.m. May 3 near Hi-Mount Community School, 4921 W. Garfield Ave. A John Doe investigation concerning her disappearance was begun in January and is ongoing.

The complaint issued Tuesday against Bourgeois accused him of beating Ayanna Patterson on April 9 after he demanded to know the identity of someone who had paged her and she professed ignorance.

"(Expletive), you know who it is!" Bourgeois insisted as he punched her "several times" in the head, according to the complaint.

"(Expletive), I'm going to kill you today.

"(Expletive), I'm going to jail today."

Eventually, according to the complaint, Bourgeois began threatening her with a knife, and she begged him not to kill her. The complaint says Ayanna Patterson phoned a friend for help and told her that she had been beaten, prompting Bourgeois to take the telephone from her and pull the cord out of the wall.

After the friend arrived to help her and his wife began packing, according to the complaint, Bourgeois continued to berate her.

When Bourgeois spoke with police later, according to the complaint, he said that he and his wife "have been constantly arguing lately" and he wanted to separate from her for a while.

Bourgeois

The truth about his character was exposed to the world in this incident

One year later, fervor to find Alexis wanes

By REID J. EPSTEIN
repstein@journalsentinel.com

It's been a year since Alexis Patterson disappeared, but authorities are no closer to finding the 8-year-old than they were when she vanished.

While leads still come in — roughly one a month — Milwaukee police have five detectives searching for the girl. However, as the months pass, the citizens group formed to help search for Alexis has mostly disbanded and the Sheriff's Department says it is no longer involved in the search.

Police Chief Arthur Jones said he does not know what the Police Department could have done differently in its searches, but he insisted that the case will be solved.

"Because of efforts we've made in the past and efforts we'll make in the future, we will find out what happened to her," Jones said.

A source said MPD receives tips from people who claim to have seen Alexis and psychics who report visions about where she has been. MPD checks out all tips — including one two months ago that placed Alexis at a house in Chicago. There was no proof that she was ever there.

A John Doe investigation into the girl's disappearance began in Milwaukee County Circuit Court on Jan. 3. Because those subpoenaed to testify at these proceedings

Please see ALEXIS, 2B

MISSING
ALEXIS PATTERSON TIMELINE

MISSING PERSO[N]
MILWAUKEE COUNTY SHERIFF
David A. Clarke Jr. Sheriff

PATTERSON, ALEXIS

Police 'no closer' to finding Alexis Patterson 1 year later

In this article they refer to psychics that had visions of Alexis whereabouts. One of them was John Claud. A guy I mentioned in the book. They kept his name out the article.

157

Murdered girl had a familiar face

Family feared child was Alexis Patterson

By JESSICA MCBRIDE
jmcbride@journalsentinel.com

The photograph of the murdered girl from Georgia looked a lot like Alexis Patterson, who disappeared from Milwaukee last year.

Same bright eyes Same broad smile. Roughly the same age as Alexis would be today.

It turns out that Joella Reaves, 11, was not Alexis Patterson, who disappeared in May 2002 after her stepfather walked her to Hi-Mount Elementary School, 4921 W. Garfield Ave.

But the striking resemblance convinced Alexis' family members for days this week that the girls were one

Alexis

Joella

and the same, sending the relatives tumbling into a mixture of hope and despair.

At the very least, they thought, the two girls were doppelgangers.

"It was something else," Levoria Aikens, Alexis' maternal grandmother, said Friday. "It looked just like her. I was just praying it wasn't "

Georgia authorities have charged Joella's father and stepmother with tying her up and battering her at their home near Atlanta over the

Thanksgiving holiday The girl was found dead Dec 1

Rene Swanson, the lead detective investigating Joella's death with the Henry County Police Department in Georgia, said two Milwaukee police detectives contacted her about the resemblance right after Joella was found Dec 1

Swanson said she has a record trail on Joella that dates to well before Alexis disappeared. "She lived with her maternal aunt along with another sibling "

A relative of Alexis' saw Joella's picture online — the slaying has garnered national media attention — leading Aikens and other family members to think the girl could be Alexis.

"I did (think Joella was Alexis)." Aikens said "The facial It looked like her, like she was a little older And

with her being gone for a year, kids mature real fast."

Two of Alexis' great-aunts went to Milwaukee police with the information Thursday night, not knowing police had already ruled it out.

"The little girl resembles Alexis so much — it has to be her They are too identical," Loretta Hubbert, Alexis' great-aunt, said before learning it was not

Alexis' relatives were relieved to hear they were mistaken "Oh, Lord, yes. That's good This was the closest call," Aikens said after learning police had ruled out the possibility the dead child was Alexis.

Anyone who may have information about Alexis Patterson is asked to call the Milwaukee Police Department's Sensitive Crimes Division at (414) 935-7401 or (414) 935-7302

This was a sad ordeal involving Joella. I was very relieved to learn that it was not Alexis, but I would have never used the words "that's good" to describe how I felt after learning that it wasn't Alexis. I still have and show empathy towards Joella's family whose experiencing turmoil like myself.

cases in cards

Agency to distribute photos in decks in hopes of new leads

By EMMA ROLLER
eroller@journalsentinel.com

Madison — The state Department of Justice is using a creative strategy in hopes of uncovering new information on unsolved homicides and missing persons in Wisconsin: distributing playing cards with pictures of the victims' faces and descriptions of the cold cases.

The cards will be distributed to prisons and sheriff's departments throughout the state in the hopes that inmates will recognize information on the cards and come forward with a lead.

Two decks of playing cards are being released — one for Milwaukee-area cases and one for the rest of the state. The cases span from 1953 to 2008.

"The information received from an inmate might just be the missing link that can breathe new life into a case that has gone cold," Special Agent Jim Holmes said in a statement released by the DOJ.

Alexis Patterson, the 7-year-old Milwaukee girl whose disappearance in 2002 dominated headlines in the city, is featured in the deck, along with Brittany Zimmermann, the 21-year-old University of Wisconsin-Madison student who was found dead in her apartment in 2008.

The DOJ says there are hundreds more cold cases in Wisconsin not included in the two decks.

Holmes, who is heading up the project, said local law enforcement agencies contacted victims' families to tell them about the initiative and requested permission to use photos of the victims on the cards.

"Some of the families were just happy that the local agencies didn't forget about the case," Holmes said.

Similar programs exist in Florida, Indiana, Minnesota, Missouri, Texas and Washington. The Wisconsin project was funded through donations from various law enforcement associations in the state along with a national grant from the U.S. Department of Justice's National Institute of Justice.

It cost $10,500 to produce the initial 2,000 decks of cards for the program. Of that, 800 decks were given to the Department of Corrections to distribute throughout the state's prisons.

Patricia Clason, a member of Mar-

Please see CARDS, 5B

From page 1

CARDS

Decks sent to prisons

quette University Law School's Restorative Justice Initiative, said having unmarked cards identifying cold-case victims is a good idea, but said it is tasteless to make playing cards with victims' faces on them.

"To see this information on a playing card with the king of hearts on it ... that's a possi-

bility of emotional damage Clason said. "It's inappropriate; it's insensitive and it's disrespectful."

Holmes said seeing the victim on the card can "really hit home" with prisoners who may come forward with information.

"It really personalizes the case," Holmes said.

Cold case cards distributed

The state Department of Justice is releasing two decks of playing cards highlighting unsolved homicides and missing persons cases. One set is for the Milwaukee area and one is for the rest of the state. Both sets are being distributed statewide to prisons and sheriff's offices in hopes of sparking leads. Evelyn Hartley (lower left) is the oldest cold case, while Jane Doe (lower right) is one of the more recent cases.

7 MISSING PERSON
ALEXIS PATTERSON
(7-Years-Old at time of disappearance)

Alexis Patterson was last seen on May 3rd, 2002, at approximately 8:00 AM, walking from her home at 2218 N. 49th St. in Milwaukee to Hi Mount Elementary School at 4921 W. Garfield Ave. Alexis was last seen wearing a red jacket, a blue and grey-striped shirt, and blue jean pants.

Please call the Milwaukee Police Department at (414) 935-1212 if you have any information regarding this case.

2 UNSOLVED HOMICIDE
KEONTAY WATSON
(29-Years-Old)

During the early morning hours on Monday, June 15, 2008, Keontay Watson was standing in the 900 block of Hamilton Street in Racine, Wisconsin, at which time, he was shot in what appeared to be a drive-by shooting. Watson was transported to the hospital for treatment; however he later succumbed to his injuries.

Please call the Racine Police Department at 262-635-9330 if you having any information regarding this case.

4 MISSING PERSON/PRESUMED VICTIM OF HOMICIDE
EVELYN HARTLEY
(15-Years-Old)

On October 24, 1953, Evelyn Hartley was babysitting at a home in the 2400 block of Hoeschler Drive, located on the south side of La Crosse, Wisconsin. Evelyn was presumably kidnapped and she has never been heard from since. Evelyn's body has never been found.

If you have any information regarding this case, please contact the La Crosse Police Department at 608-785-5962.

10 RECOVERED BODY (JANE DOE)
UNIDENTIFIED FEMALE

On November 23, 2008, the Fond du Lac County Sheriff's Office recovered the remains of a female body. The body was recovered in a secluded wooded area in rural Fond du Lac County. This location is approximately half way between Fond du Lac, WI and Milwaukee, WI. The body was partially decomposed and clothed in blue jeans and a black top with pink trim at the time of discovery.

If you have any information regarding this case call the Fond du Lac County Sheriff's Tip Line at (920) 906-4777

Source: State Department of Justice

Journal Sentinel

ORIN ANDERSON, 16
LAST SEEN: AUG. 28, 1973

KAYLA BERG, 15
LAST SEEN: AUG. 11, 2009

RICKY JEAN 'JEANIE' BRYANT, 4
LAST SEEN: DEC. 19, 1949

SARA BUSHLAND, 15
LAST SEEN: APRIL 3, 1996

MADELINE EDMAN, 15
LAST SEEN: JULY 29, 2005

STILL MISSING

THE LOST
PART 2 OF 2

BOBBY JOE FRITZ, 5
LAST SEEN: MAY 14, 1983

EVELYN HARTLEY, 15
LAST SEEN: OCT. 24, 1953

DONTRAY MIQUEL HUNTER, 1
LAST SEEN: AUG. 20, 1975

MACKENZIE MARKEN, 14
LAST SEEN: OCT. 11, 2015

ALEXIS PATTERSON, 7
LAST SEEN: MAY 3, 2002

CATHY SJOBERG, 17
LAST SEEN: JUNE 5, 1974

ALEXIS NANETTE CONLEY-WADE, 15
LAST SEEN: JUNE 26, 2014

GEORGIA WECKLER, 8
LAST SEEN: MAY 1, 1947

ALEXIS PATTERSON

Age: 7
Last seen: May 3, 2002
Investigative contact: Milwaukee Police Detective Kathy Spano, 414-933-4444

Summary: Milwaukee's most high-profile missing child is Alexis Patterson. It's been 15 years since she vanished between her home and her neighborhood school. Her stepfather, LaRon Bourgeois, told Milwaukee police that he walked the child to elementary school and last saw her crossing the street near the school, according to Journal Sentinel reports. Alexis' mother called police after her 7-year-old daughter did not return home from school that day. School officials determined that Alexis did not show up for class that day. Bourgeois has been questioned and denied involvement in the girl's disappearance.

Patterson

Alexis and other missing children featured in the Post-Crescent paper from Appleton, WI. March 20, 2017.

New hope in disappearance

Officials trying to determine if Ohio woman is Alexis Patterson

By CROCKER STEPHENSON
cstephenson@journalsentinel.com

Law enforcement officials are trying to determine if a woman living in Ohio is Alexis Patterson, the Milwaukee girl who vanished 14 years ago, a mystery that remains an open wound to those touched by her story.

Questions about the Ohio woman arose when the woman's ex-husband and his fiancée became increasingly curious about her murky past.

Patterson
in 2002

The woman, they say, has no memory of her childhood before the age of 10. She has no photographs or school mementos — indeed, no usual reminders of a

Please see **PATTERSON, 7A**

162

From page 1
PATTERSON

New hope in 2002 disappearance of Milwaukee girl

normal childhood.

That was enough to spur the ex-husband and fiancée to search for clues on the internet. They came upon a computer-aged photograph of Alexis Patterson, and became convinced that Alexis is the woman they know.

The couple compiled a set of about a dozen photos and, in late June, sent it to the Milwaukee County Sheriff's Department. Within days, they also sent it to the Journal Sentinel, hoping for action.

The Journal Sentinel shared the photos with the Milwaukee Police Department's cold case unit, which has been in charge of Alexis' case since 2009.

Alexis' mother, Ayanna Patterson, has never wavered in her belief that her daughter is alive. But she has had her hopes built up by purported breaks in her daughter's case, only to have them crash when the breaks didn't pan out. She has been besieged by hustlers claiming to know her daughter or even to be her daughter.

When the Journal Sentinel showed her the photos, Patterson's initial skepticism gave way to cautious optimism.

"That could be my baby," she said when she first examined the photographs. "I've never said this before, but that could be my child."

Her optimism deepened when the Journal Sentinel traveled to Ohio and interviewed the couple.

The woman, they said, has two features often mentioned in descriptions of Alexis by such organizations as the FBI and the National Center for Missing and Exploited Children: a linear scar beneath her right eye and an unusual bump on her left pinkie finger.

They also mentioned a third characteristic, one that has not been released to the general public. When the Journal Sentinel contacted Ayanna Patterson, she confirmed that Alexis had that characteristic. And then she wept.

There are numerous rea-

sons to doubt that the woman is Alexis, chief among them her age. The woman says she is 28 — seven years older than Alexis would be — and she has two children.

For her to be Alexis, she would have given birth at an unusually young age. She remembers being brought to California and living in various locations, but has no memory, according to her ex-husband, of Milwaukee or any connection to people or places here.

The Journal Sentinel is not identifying the ex-husband, his fiancée or the woman they suspect may be Alexis to protect their privacy and the integrity of the investigation.

Word that Milwaukee police were headed to Ohio to collect DNA samples was made public Friday without the knowledge of the family in Milwaukee or the couple in Ohio. Several TV stations cited Milwaukee police as their source.

But it appears DNA samples had already been taken. After hearing from a frustrated Ayanna Patterson, state Rep. Lena Taylor had contacted several agencies and officials seeking help with the case. The Sheriff's Office responded, Taylor said.

Law enforcement officials would not say how quickly results of the genetic test will be ready.

Without a trace

Alexis went missing May 3, 2002.

A slight 7-year-old with a photogenic grin, her hair beaded and twisted into French braids and ponytails, Alexis lived just around the corner from her school, Hi-Mount Community, 4921 W. Garfield Ave.

Her stepfather, LaRon Bourgeois, told police he watched her walk toward the school that morning and that the last time he saw her, about 8 a.m., she was at the crosswalk.

Ayanna Patterson called the police about 3 p.m. to tell them her daughter hadn't come home. Her teachers subsequently said they had not

163

There are numerous rea-

come home. Her teachers sub- sequently said they had not seen her in class.

Milwaukee police, joined by the Sheriff's Office and other metro-area law enforcement personnel, conducted an intensive search. Hundreds of volunteers, on foot and bicycle, joined the hunt. An image of a smiling Alexis was posted throughout the city.

"I care about Alexis Patterson," then-Police Chief Arthur Jones told people gathered for a vigil 10 days after the child vanished.

"The Milwaukee Police Department cares about Alexis Patterson," he said. "The case of Alexis Patterson will not be closed until she is found."

On the 10th anniversary of Alexis' disappearance, Lt. Keith Balash, commander of the Police Department's Cold Case Unit, announced that investigators had conducted 5,000 interviews, had compiled a case file more than 10,000 pages long and had repeatedly traveled out of state in search of the child.

The unit developed a cold case deck of cards, which was

distributed to prisons throughout Wisconsin, in the hopes that an inmate might recognize the child and share any information about her. Alexis was the seven of hearts.

"The Milwaukee Police Department would like to emphasize to the community, to the parents, family, relatives and friends that this case is still actively being investigated by dedicated and experienced investigators," Balash said at the time.

Red flags

The Ohio woman and her ex-husband were married in August 2009, had a son and divorced after three years. At the time of their marriage, the woman had a daughter from an earlier relationship.

In an interview with the Journal Sentinel, the ex-husband said the woman told him she had been born in Central America on Valentine's Day 1988, that she was abandoned by her father, and that she was brought to the United States by her mother and stepfather about 12 years ago.

Further, the ex-husband said the woman did not initially have a birth certificate. One had to be purchased from the country where she believes she was born before they could marry.

The date of birth on the certificate — if it is real — would mean the Ohio woman is seven years older than Alexis. Such an incongruity in age is difficult to explain, said Milwaukee cold case Detective Erik Villarreal.

"The dates of birth make it very unlikely this is her," he said.

But Ayanna Patterson's initial skepticism has evolved into a deeply felt certainty.

"My heart is telling me this is my child," she said. "My baby is coming home."

But what if the genetic test proves otherwise?

"I am strong," she said. "I will keep looking."

I was praying that young lady from Ohio was Alexis when this story broke in July of 2016. I was so excited and optimistic.

No match to Alexis

DNA results show Ohio woman not girl who vanished in 2002

By CROCKER STEPHENSON
cstephenson@journalsentinel.com

The results of genetic testing released Thursday exclude the possibility that an Ohio woman is Alexis Patterson, the Milwaukee girl who vanished on her way to school 14 years ago.

Alexis' mother, Ayanna Patterson, reacted with grief, rage, disbelief — as well as sadness for the Ohio woman who, her daughter or not, has endured intense scrutiny by the media and by people living in her small town.

"No matter what the test says, I still believe one billion percent you are my child," Patterson told the Journal Sentinel, as if speaking to the Ohio woman.

Patterson herself has been exposed to similar scrutiny, which she has found painful, and has avoided returning to her home. She met with the Journal Sentinel at a park on the city's far north side.

"I want you to continue to go on with your life and be as happy as you can be," Patterson said of the Ohio woman. "And be the best mother you can possibly be. And raise your children. And don't let no one hurt your kids. Don't let your children out of your sight.

"I know you are hurting right now," Patterson said. "And I am sorry."

In a statement, Milwaukee police officials said they

From page 1

ALEXIS
DNA test disproves genetic link

3, 2002. The 7-year-old girl lived just around the corner from her school, Hi-Mount Community, 4921 W. Garfield Ave.

Her stepfather, LaRon Bourgeois, told police he watched her walk toward the school that morning and that the last time he saw her, about 8 a.m., she was at the crosswalk.

Ayanna Patterson called the police about 3 p.m. to tell them her daughter had not come home. Her teachers said Alexis was not in class earlier that day. Hundreds of volunteers joined law enforcement officers in a search for Alexis and posters with her image were posted across the city.

While the Ohio woman

shared several characteristics peculiar to Alexis, there were several reasons Milwaukee police doubted they were one in the same.

The woman says she is 28 — seven years older than Alexis would be — and she has two children. For her to be Alexis, she would have given birth at an unusually young age.

Ayanna Patterson said she was not satisfied with the DNA results. The 14-year-old samples may be corrupted or have deteriorated over the years.

"I don't believe that DNA test," she said.

She demanded investigators run another test, this time comparing the Ohio woman's DNA to her own, which she provided to police

on Wednesday.

"Prove me wrong," she said. "Make it clear to me."

Asked if investigators would consider conducting another test, the Police Department replied in a statement: "We are absolutely sure it is not her based on DNA."

"They don't understand what I've been going through for 14 years," Patterson said. "I worry about my daughter everyday. I've worried about my daughter for 14 years.

"This is my pain."

Patterson said she will continue to pressure the police to conduct a test using her DNA.

"I'm not going to stop."

Journal Sentinel reporter Ashley Luthern contributed to this report.

"received a call from the Wisconsin Regional Crime Lab regarding the results of DNA testing derived from a tip from an Ohio man relative to the 2002 disappearance of Alexis Patterson.

"The sample collected by law enforcement authorities in Ohio of a female there does NOT match that of Patterson's."

The man referred to in the statement is the Ohio woman's ex-husband, who, with his fiancée, became increasingly curious about the woman's seemingly murky past.

Struck by the woman's resemblance to age-progressed images of Alexis, the couple compiled a set of about a dozen photos and

sent it to the Milwaukee County Sheriff's Office in late June.

Days later, they also sent the photos to the Journal Sentinel, which shared the photos with the Milwaukee Police Department's cold case unit.

Alexis went missing May

Please see ALEXIS, 6A

A week after the young lady was tested for a genetic link, the results of the DNA test proved that she wasn't Alexis. I was saddened and confused. Sad because it wasn't my daughter and confused because the police used a 14 year old toothbrush and not fresh blood or saliva from her mother or myself.

USA TODAY

THE NATION'S NEWS | $2 | TUESDAY, MAY 3, 2022

CINDY ORD/C

Two missing children, two different outcomes

They vanished a month apart, but similarity ends there

Alexis Patterson was 7 when she vanished; Elizabeth Smart was 14. Twenty years later, Alexis is still missing.
PHOTOS PROVIDED BY FAMILIES

Gina Barton and Ashley Luthern

USA TODAY NETWORK

On the morning of May 3, 2002, Alexis Patterson's stepfather walked her to the corner and a crossing guard guided the 7-year-old across the street toward Hi-Mount Community School in Milwaukee. At the end of the day, she didn't come home.

A month later and more than a thousand miles away, Elizabeth Smart, 14, went to sleep in her bedroom in Salt Lake City. By the next morning, she was gone.

Within hours, Elizabeth's disappearance was featured on CNN's "Larry King Live" and Fox News' "On the Record with Greta Van Susteren." It took eight days for Alexis' story to attract attention outside Milwaukee, with a segment on "America's Most Wanted." The next national story on her case aired weeks later.

By the time Elizabeth had been gone two weeks, USA TODAY had published three stories about her disappearance. There were none focused on Alexis.

Help USA TODAY investigate disparities in cases of missing children

If you know of missing children of color in your community or have experienced these disparities firsthand as a parent, friend or law enforcement officer, we want to hear from you. Visit **bit.ly/usatoday-missing-tips**.

The law enforcement response also differed. The day after Elizabeth disappeared, police called in the FBI and offered a $250,000 reward. In Milwaukee, the FBI didn't join Alexis' case until three days after she vanished. Nineteen days after she was last seen, the sheriff's office offered a $10,000 reward.

Elizabeth is white. She was found nine months after her abduction. Alexis is Black – and still missing.

Twenty years ago, as police searched for the two girls, some advocates and experts argued that race was a key factor in how authorities and reporters handled their cases. It marked the first time the national media paid serious attention to such disparities.

Two years later, Black journalist Gwen Ifill gave the phenomenon a name: "missing white woman syndrome." She coined the term after the disappearance of Laci Peterson, a pregnant California woman whose husband was later convicted of kill-

See MISSING, Page 6A

If Hussein can be found, surely so can Alexis

It would have been a blockbuster of a story.

Alexis Patterson, found, after all this time.

But, if the suspicions had turned out to be correct, it would have been a terrible story, too.

Alexis would have been found, but she would have been dead.

And that would have been the most tragic conclusion to the mystery that has confounded Milwaukee for more than a year and a half now.

EUGENE KANE

As most remember, 7-year-old Alexis disappeared in May 2002 after being walked to her elementary school by her stepfather.

Since then, nobody knows what happened to her. It's like she dropped off the face of the earth.

But a photograph of an 11-year-old Georgia girl who was found dead on Dec. 1 and made the national news looked so familiar to some, it set off a whirlwind of speculation.

Members of Alexis' family and others who saw the picture online were convinced it might be Alexis.

They started calling the media and the police. Because the face was so familiar, the smile and those eyes.

It certainly seemed worth a shot.

I received a call from someone convinced the media needed to check out "this dead girl in Georgia" who looked so much like Alexis.

Sure, the dead girl in Georgia was 11 years old; Alexis would be only 8 by now. But most people with children understand the subtle and not-so-subtle ways a child can mature over a year and a half.

Again, maybe it was worth something.

Authorities here and in Georgia looked into the matter and were convinced it wasn't Alexis. The face belonged to Joella Reaves, who was beaten to death. Her father and stepmother have been charged with her death.

Thankfully, it wasn't Alexis. Not so thankfully, we're back where we started.

It's not like hoping for some resolution into Alexis' disappearance after all this time is a futile quest. After all, they found Saddam Hussein last weekend, one bushy-haired guy hiding out in a vast country.

They are still searching for Dru Sjodin, the 22-year-old University of North Dakota student who vanished on Nov. 22 after leaving her job at a Victoria's Secret store in a Grand Forks mall.

A likely suspect — a convicted sex offender — is in custody, and there is enough evidence so far to allow authorities to say she's most likely dead, even as her friends and family hold out hope.

Alexis

When Alexis disappeared, there was a slow response to her plight, particularly from the national media who were so fixated over the kidnapping of Elizabeth Smart in Salt Lake City that they neglected to notice a missing black child in the Midwest.

Unlike in the Smart and Sjodin cases, Alexis' parents — stepfather LaRon Bourgeois and her mother, Ayanna Patterson — didn't choose to give daily news conferences or provide regular updates for the media.

While citizens who didn't even know Alexis fanned out in volunteer search parties and support organizations, her parents appeared to recede from the spotlight, perhaps due to the stepfather's legal troubles, which made him an early suspect.

In May, Bourgeois was charged with battery and disorderly conduct over accusations he beat Alexis' mother. He is in jail awaiting trial on those charges.

Whispers about Alexis' disappearance still come into the Journal Sentinel newsroom from time to time. I've heard everything from her being kidnapped and taken to Mexico to speculation that she's living a secluded new life in Chicago.

Somebody told me once she was in upstate Wisconsin, living on a farm.

Any of those would be preferable to discovering that she met the same fate as her look-alike in Georgia.

If Alexis' face had been plastered nationally like Elizabeth Smart's in those first few days, who knows what leads might have been uncovered.

But that's not the battle to fight

anymore, the debate over whether the media gravitates to the image of blond white girls from affluent families more than a black child from the central city.

These days, it's just about finding a final chapter to this baffling story.

The morning they found Hussein, I found myself thinking that maybe it will happen the same way with Alexis. One morning, you wake up and the local news will be telling the story of her discovery, hopefully alive and well.

If not, at least there will be some sort of closure for her family and the community that grew to love her once she was gone.

Little girls just don't fall off the face of the earth, no more than harsh dictators do.

Something happened to Alexis Patterson, the missing little girl we can't get out of our minds.

We do know that, for a fact.

Call Eugene Kane at (414) 223-5521 or e-mail him at ekane@journalsentinel.com.

I feel somethings are better off not said, but I will say this, when Central City was mentioned in this article, what it really was saying was the ghetto. This article speaks volume and I'll leave it at that.

Alexis Patterson at age 7 (left) and as she might look today.

Have you seen this girl?

Five years ago Thursday, 7-year-old Alexis Patterson of Milwaukee went off to school and never got there, prompting one of the biggest searches in Milwaukee history. Today, efforts to find her continue. A computer-enhanced photo of what Alexis might look like today (above, right) is from the National Center for Missing and Exploited Children, *www.missingkids.com.* **1B**

Abducted Utah teen is found alive

ELIZABETH, From 1A

very excited. It was the kind of reunion you would expect."

Speaking to reporters later, Elizabeth's father, Ed, a real estate developer, said, tearfully: "I am so happy. I am so grateful for the prayers, the help and the eyes out there. It's so wonderful."

He said, "I don't know what she's gone through and I'm sure she's been through hell. I just know that she's a part of our family, she's loved and we love her so much."

He said she "looks very, very healthy. She's grown a lot. She is so thrilled to be back."

Elizabeth was returned home about 9:20 p.m. CST in an unmarked police van. She did not speak to reporters as she rushed inside the house.

In the Federal Heights neighborhood where the Smarts live, signs sprang up within minutes of Elizabeth's recovery, saying, "Welcome Home" and "We Love You." Blue and yellow balloons went up everywhere. Neighbors hugged and cried.

Spotted by two couples

Police were tipped off by members of the public who spotted Mitchell on a street in Sandy. Mitchell, Barzee and Elizabeth were all wearing wigs, authorities said, adding that Barzee and Elizabeth had blue, pillowcase-like veils over their faces.

Relatives of Mitchell have described him as a self-appointed prophet for the homeless who lived in a tepee in mountains outside the city. He was hired by the Smarts in November 2001 to work on their roof.

A Smart family spokesman, Chris Thomas, said Elizabeth apparently had no chance to escape. "She said there was no way, she had two people with her at all times," he said.

Police stopped Mitchell and the others after receiving calls a minute apart from Rudy and Nancy Montoya and Anita and Alvin Dickerson. Both couples had spotted the trio carrying bedrolls and bags as they walked down the street.

Anita Dickerson, thinking the man resembled the suspect, left her car and looked him in the eye. She thought Elizabeth was an older woman wearing a scarf.

"Lots of people had to see them, they just didn't put two and two together," Alvin Dickerson said.

Tom Smart said: "Absolutely, it's a miracle. ... The odds that they happen are extreme, but I don't think any little girl was prayed for more in the history of the world."

'Camped and traveled'

Dinse declined to discuss any details of Elizabeth's 9-month ordeal.

Thomas said that for part of the time, Elizabeth "camped and traveled around to different parts of the country."

Police said that they are investigating whether she had spent part of the months since her June 5 abduction living on the road with her alleged kidnappers and traveling as far as San Diego and south Florida.

Mayor Ross C. Anderson called it "a great day for the people of Salt Lake City and throughout the nation." He praised the fortitude of Elizabeth's parents, Ed and Lois, who never doubted their daughter still was alive, and thanked all those who prayed for her safe return, saying of the Smarts that "they believe those prayers were answered today."

The discovery of Elizabeth, who was 14 when she disappeared, came as a stunning conclusion to a case that mystified investigators throughout Utah and devastated a family that nonetheless always insisted that she would be found alive.

At the time of her disappearance last summer, she was the latest in a chilling series of child abductions that included those of Danielle van Dam, of San Diego and Samantha

ASSOCIATED PRESS

Anita and Alvin Dickerson, the couple who called police in Sandy, Utah, after recognizing "Emmanuel," answer questions during a news conference Wednesday in Salt Lake City.

Brian David Mitchell, the suspect, is shown in these 2002, 2000 and 1998 photos (left to right) and in a sketch that the Smart family released.

Alexis' case still being investigated

By ALLISON L. SMITH
alsmith@journalsentinel.com

A Utah teenager's rescue months after she was kidnapped at gunpoint has barely fanned a spark of hope for a similar happy ending in the case of Alexis Patterson, the 7-year-old Milwaukee girl who vanished on her way to school 10 months ago.

Milwaukee police Capt. Brian O'Keefe, who has spearheaded the police search for the girl, declined to comment Wednesday on how news of Smart's recovery in Utah might affect hope for finding Alexis.

"All I will say is that our investigation is still active," O'Keefe said.

Operation L.A.P. (Locate Alexis Patterson), a local volunteer group, disbanded in November after money ran out in the search for the girl and public interest waned. The group's founder, Keith Martin, could not be reached for comment Wednesday.

Likewise, Alexis' stepfather and mother, Ayanna Patterson Bourgeois, could not be located for comment Wednesday night.

Alexis was last seen the morning of May 3, when her stepfather, LaRon Bourgeois, walked her a half-block from their former home to Hi-Mount Elementary School, 4921 W. Garfield Ave.

Alexis:
Missing since May 3.

Ricci

Runion, 5, of Orange County, Calif., both of whom were later found murdered.

Throughout much of the investigation, the police in Salt Lake City focused attention on Richard A. Ricci, another handyman who had worked at the Smart home. He was arrested on a parole violation last summer and died in jail after suffering a cerebral hemorrhage in August. Ricci, and his wife, Angela, always insisted that he had nothing to do with the girl's disappearance.

Members of the Smart family frequently expressed skepticism that

Ricci had any involvement in Elizabeth's abduction.

The family's divergent belief was based on the account of the only eyewitness in the case, Elizabeth's 9-year-old sister, Mary Katherine, who shared the same bedroom and pretended to be asleep, as she told authorities, when Elizabeth was led away at gunpoint. Mary Katherine said that the man threatened to harm Elizabeth if her younger sister made any noise or notified her parents, asleep in another room.

At one point last fall, Ed Smart said, Mary Katherine came to her parents and said, "Daddy, I think I know who it might be," and she identified a man who worked at the home. The family hired the man, whom they came to know as Emmanuel, after Lois Smart encountered him panhandling on a downtown Salt Lake City street.

Little is known about the couple now in police custody. Mitchell has been variously described as a drifter and handyman with deep religious beliefs.

Mitchell's stepsons, Mark and Derek Thompson, had little good to say about their stepfather and their mother. They said their mother and Mitchell have been married for more than 16 years and, as devout Mormons, consider themselves prophets who speak directly to God.

Mark Thompson, 32, a construction worker in Salt Lake City, said in a telephone interview that when his younger sister was 14, she chose to live with her father, rather than her mother and Mitchell. He suggested that that broke his mother's spirit, saying: "I'm mom just freaked out then, and I remember her saying, 'How dare my baby leave me.' Maybe she felt like she needed to replace a child."

Thompson said his mother carried around dolls of babies and girls for years, pretending they were alive. He said she has also been forcibly removed from a local hospital — as recently as last year — "for touching other people's kids."

"We just knew it was him," Mark Thompson said. "I've never liked the guy and felt he's always had something to do with this."

Don't forget missing local girl, police say

By KELLY WELLS
kwells@journalsentinel.com

Milwaukee police said Thursday that although the case of Elizabeth Smart came to a "great conclusion," people in Milwaukee should not forget Alexis Patterson, the 7-year-old girl who has been missing for 10 months.

At a media question and answer session hosted by the Milwaukee bureau of the FBI, Assistant Police Chief Edward Stenzel said authorities are still actively investigating Alexis' case and are keeping in touch with her parents but have no suspects. Police have no evidence that suggests the girl's parents played any role in her disappearance, he said.

Alexis

Stenzel pointed out that although the safe return of the Utah teenager provides hope that Alexis could be found, the cases are substantially different because police had a suspect in Smart's case.

David Mitchell, FBI special agent in charge, agreed with Stenzel.

"This was a clear-cut abduction," Mitchell said of Smart's disappearance. "It's a different case."

Stenzel said the department has followed "hundreds of leads" and conducted more than 2,700 interviews in the Alexis investigation. The department is handling the case as intensely as it has from the beginning, he said, though the number of people assigned to it varies depending on new information.

The FBI is still involved, too, Mitchell said.

Stenzel refused to comment on the John Doe investigation into Alexis' disappearance.

Alexis was last seen on May 3 when her stepfather, LaRon Bourgeois, walked her to Hi-Mount Elementary School, 4921 W. Garfield Ave.

172

SO YOU CAN WRITE
PUBLICATIONS®

"Where the writers go…"
www.sycwp.com

www.ingramcontent.com/pod-product-compliance
Lightning Source LLC
Chambersburg PA
CBHW072247270326
41930CB00010B/2295